About the Author

Michael Nelson is a courageous fighter, and an honest person. She hates hypocrisy and doesn't hesitate to bring up the only language they know. Namely sincerity. She is loyal and firm in her convictions. She needs to know the person in front of her and that she loves to respect her as a friend or co-worker is genuine, genuine at all times. She has a master's degree in European and International law. Her hobbies: Pray, play tennis, read, and write books.

Racism: A Problematic

Racism: A Problematic

Michael Nelson

Racism: A Problematic

Olympia Publishers
London

www.olympiapublishers.com
OLYMPIA PAPERBACK EDITION

Copyright © Michael Nelson 2023

The right of Michael Nelson to be identified as author of
this work has been asserted in accordance with sections 77 and 78 of
the Copyright, Designs and Patents Act 1988.

All Rights Reserved

No reproduction, copy or transmission of this publication
may be made without written permission.
No paragraph of this publication may be reproduced,
copied or transmitted save with the written permission of the publisher,
or in accordance with the provisions
of the Copyright Act 1956 (as amended).

Any person who commits any unauthorised act in relation to
this publication may be liable to criminal
prosecution and civil claims for damage.

A CIP catalogue record for this title is
available from the British Library.

ISBN: 978-1-80074-484-4

First Published in 2023

Olympia Publishers
Tallis House
2 Tallis Street
London
EC4Y 0AB

Printed in Great Britain

Dedication

I dedicate this book to targeted victims of racism, and to those who suffer unacceptable silence in the shadows.

For all people who have suffered from the actions of oppressors, regardless of their size, they are assigned to frighten, destabilize, discriminate, despise, evaluate, abuse, punish, humiliate, oppress and destroy the weak. First of all, I want to thank the supreme man, who has been everywhere in my life, and guided me to make all decisions, and let me write this book. Special thanks to my children, who believe in my potential and are always by my side.

For all those who do not support destabilization, racist oppression.

Preface

Colonization and Racism, no matter what language you speak, two big words. These two words quickly covered the entire colonial situation. Indeed, the reflection on colonization is directed at the debates about discrimination and racism in French society, and the debate has become a historical background: the contemporary forms of social problems will be racial because they will find their origins in practice and thought patterns. Colonial period: a difficult period, a period of turbulence, a period of oppression that the victim will not forget. Why does this happen for what reason? Is there a place in the world that says that black people have to become slaves because of their culture, skin color, ideas, etc.?

In the debate between these discriminatory behaviors, two assumptions are at work: the racialization of social relations and colonial history. The first question concerns the history of colonial racism: in territories belonging to the sovereignty of France, especially in the colonies of modern colonial empires, Africa, Asia and the Pacific, a special form of racism. The definition of a colony is the annexation of territory by foreign troops for political and economic purposes. This action represents one of the undeniable facts in the history of the world, and it developed in a larger and larger form with the expansion of Europe in the fifteenth century.

Colonization then specified the conquest of a country's territory and its population. However, the biogeography of the nineteenth century used this term to describe this type of relationship among all living things (including animals, plants, and microorganisms) in the natural environment. Another meaning is the act of supervising the citizens of underdeveloped areas and sparsely populated metropolises. The goal of occupying it and developing its wealth. In practice, the colonization process may have economic, political, military or cultural characteristics, or manifest in other ways; it may even develop in a violent or peaceful way. Colonization can be a process of territorial or population expansion. It is characterized by a wave of immigration in the form of immigration, a more or less rapid occupation or even a brutal invasion of the territory.

In the most extreme cases, colonization may be accompanied by marginalization, massacre, and genocide. All this has to do with racism "skin color". Strictly speaking, racism is "an ideology based on the belief that there is a hierarchy among human groups," race, behavior inspired by this ideology in a broad sense is "an attitude". Being systematically hostile to a certain type of people. Some sociologists believe that racism is part of the dynamics of social domination under racial rule. Racist ideology has become the basis of political doctrines that lead to racial discrimination, apartheid and injustice and violence. In extreme cases, according to Abraham Maslow and the Hate Pyramid, genocide can lead to genocide.

Some people are talking about "reverse racism" which itself is an expression using the term "racism" but the behavior or statement it describes is not from a member of a dominant social group, but from a member of a previous groupcurrently in a dominant position and does not follow the racist ideas behind "white supremacy".

Acknowledgements

I thank Olympia Publishers. Thank you to all my family and friends for encouraging and helping me write this book.

Restore

Although certain human organizations have made every effort to combat racism, we are still talking about racism in 2021 because there is a force that does not agree to end this issue. Every black man or woman has to face this problem every day at work, school, and on the street. It can be said that it is everywhere, but many people think that this problem can no longer be solved and white people benefit from it. This is the reason why W. E. B. du Bois, an outstanding African-American intellectual, in the early twentieth century predicted that this would be the century of "color thread". In the decades that followed, the world witnessed the end of Nazism, the Holocaust, the American civil rights movement, colonialism, and apartheid, indigenous people became political participants on the international stage, the revival of racism in Europe and the terrible sight of ethnic cleansing and genocide in Bosnia and Rwanda. For a century, the "racial division" still exists, separating nations and cultures, and separating the strong from the oppressed. Even if it binds certain people together in a close ethnic community, it also binds many others to the concept. According to the Declaration of Human Rights, racism is generally abuse and is not fully accepted. The first stipulation: All human beings are born with equal dignity and rights. They have reason and conscience, and must act with each other in a brotherly spirit.

Article 2: Everyone can use all rights and freedoms

declared in this declaration without distinction, including race, color, sex, language, religion, political opinion or any other people of national or social origin, property, birth or any other forms of insight into other situations. In addition, no distinction will be made based on the political, legal or international status of the country or region in which a person is located, regardless of whether the country or region is independent, guarded, non-autonomous or subject to any sovereignty restrictions. From Article 1 to Article 10, it is obvious that everyone should enjoy their rights unconditionally. Racism is a form of discrimination based on the origin, race or race of the victim, whether it is real or perceived. Racism devalues people based on their appearance; it is attributed to the character traits, physical, and intellectual abilities of the stereotyped image.

Racism attempts to undermine human dignity and honor, incite hatred, and encourage verbal or physical violence. It tends to spread false ideas and make people conflict with each other. We must reach consensus in a multinational debate to find a solution to this problem. The centuries of colonialism in Europe, America, Africa, Australia, Oceania and Asia were justified by the attitude of "white supremacists". In the nineteenth century, the term "white man's burden" referred to the idea that white men were obliged to build society. Other "civilized" nations are widely used to prove that the imperialist policy is a noble cause. If we look back, we know the historical record of the French Revolution.

We are all human beings, no matter what your skin color, or race, we all deserve all good treatment. The theme of racism has caused a lot of chaos and even wars in the world. In the nineteenth century, racial and biological anti-Semitism flourished throughout Europe. He found a passionate theorist in

France. The first theoretician of race is undoubtedly Henri de Boulainvilliers. He began to study the myth of the conflict between "two races" that emerged in the sixteenth century and in the early eighteenth century: high-level races, Franks or Germans, will be in struggle. Oppose the inferior races of Gauls or Gallo-Romans. It clearly reflects a trend of thought that proclaims what we understand today as "biological" racism.

They found that this thought was brainwashed over time, and later accepted the lie. Racism is an ideology, starting from the assumption of the existence of intra-race. Humans believe that certain categories of people are inherently superior to other categories of people.

Therefore, it is different from racism, which starts from the same assumptions and does not consider race to be unequal. This ideology may lead to preference for a given category of people. In a strict sense, the French Larousse dictionary has two definitions of racism, namely: "an ideology based on the belief that there is a hierarchy among people, that is, race", behavior inspired by this ideology", and in a broad sense. The term means "repeated or even systematically hostile attitude towards certain categories of people." This hostility to another kind of social belonging (whether it is culture, race or simply because of skin color).

Simplicity provides many surprising benefits: your financial situation is improved, make your life simple, make a budget and execute it faithfully. Don't give up anyway. Sell the things you don't need, and only buy the things you like or need. Fewer things allow people to live in a smaller space. Taking control of your own financial situation will inevitably be more stable. Improve debt, eliminate debt, and achieve new success. Having too many financial resources can eliminate many stresses in life. The inner peace you enjoy is worth the least sacrifice. Invest, plan for the future and regain control of your finances. With a simple lifestyle, you can understand the actual situation more easily.

Your thought pressure is reduced, because it does not have to worry about it. When you understand the principles of your life, it is easier to make wise decisions. Only when you can or don't want it, you say "yes" and resolutely refuse. Take care of your body, by focusing on the most important things, your stress level will be reduced and your health will be benefitted. Stress can affect your mood, blood pressure, and mental health, to name a few. People who lead a simple life will pay attention to their health and carefully observe the health of their bodies. They care about the future so much that they should not abuse the future in the present.

Introduction

The term "racism" originated from the Nazi's project to "*Cleanse the Jews*" in Germany. However, the concept of racism existed before the word was coined. The Nazi's plan is only one stage in the long history of anti-Semitism. "Racism and Racists: Some Difficulties" looks at the origins of racism and anti-Semitism and the complexity of exploring the meaning of terms. Such inquiries raise many confusing questions and cognitive terms: racial and ethnocentrism; ethnicity, nationalism, and xenophobia; hostility or hatred towards "outsiders" and "strangers." The concept of "race" includes biological and cultural elements such as skin color, religious beliefs, and behavior.

We talk about racism every day, but these worries do not really have the motivation to solve the problem. We are all human beings, no matter what your skin color, or race, we all deserve good treatment.

The theme of racism has caused a lot of chaos and even wars in the world. In the nineteenth century, racial and biological, Anti-Semitism flourished throughout Europe. He found an enthusiastic theorist in France. The first theorist of race is undoubtedly Henri de Boulainvilliers. He began to study the myth of the conflict between "two races" that appeared in the sixteenth century and in the early eighteenth century: high-level races, Franks or Germans, will be in trouble. Oppose the inferior races of Gauls or Gallo- Romans. It clearly reflects a trend of thought that proclaims what we understand today as "biological" racism. They found that this thought was brainwashed over time, and the latter accepted the lie.

However, it was not until the 1930s when Leon Trotsky used the adjectives "racist" and "racism" in his *History of the Russian Revolution* that France began to use these names. This kind of vocabulary, its cultural meaning is to make the traditionalist Slavs qualified to defend their own culture and national lifestyle. These two words first entered the French Larousse dictionary in 1932. In the nineteenth century, this aristocratic racism merged with descriptive anthropology, based on the desire to define, classify, and even measure all variants of human beings, which was very typical at the time. Germany or the United States.

In France, the key milestone was Arthur de Gobineau's essay on human inequality, published between 1853 and 1855. However, it is necessary to point out the shift in employers and racism in 2021. So far, there is no solution, and concrete sanctions will be adopted to end racism. Some people may not accept the truth about racism, and officials still have not used the necessary strategies to end this scourge. In Europe, racism is developing rapidly like other countries in the world. However, administrative procedures should prove that the measures taken are effective and can lead to overall success.

Racism is an ideology, starting from the assumption of the existence of intra-race. Humans believe that certain categories of people are inherently superior to others. Therefore, it is different from racism, which starts from the same assumptions and does not consider race to be unequal. This ideology may lead to preference for a given category of people. In a strict sense, the French Larousse dictionary has two definitions of racism, namely, "an ideology based on the belief that there is a hierarchy among people, that is, race"; behavior inspired by this ideology", and in a broad sense The term "repeated or even systematically hostile attitude towards certain categories of people." This hostility to another social relationship (whether the difference is culture, race or simply due to skin color).

Racism and Dominance

There are many humanitarian organizations, and I asked myself who is willing to debate. A real conversation. It seems that many headquarters tried to solve this problem, but failed due to economic interests. Although they keep in mind the history of the racist era of blacks, it is a good thing for those who have benefited from racism. Mireille Fanon-Mendes, chairperson of the United Nations Working Group of Experts on People of African Descent, said at a special event at the United Nations Headquarters on "Facing Silence: Perspectives and Dialogues on Structural Racism for People of African Descent Around the World", the attack on human dignity was due to " The assumed hierarchy of race and culture involves not only one or the other, but also the entire international community," so it is elaborated.

The discussion was organized by the Office of the United Nations High Commissioner for Human Rights, in her speech, Ms. Fanon Mendes said that in addition to the historical consequences that African Americans have to face, they and Africans caused by colonialism, economic immigration or war are the only people who suffer from color discrimination; they are completely free from this. The biological parameters of the control of the victims of rejection. She added: "Racial hierarchy is scientifically wrong, morally condemnable, and socially unjust." She urged Member States to reverse the "invisible and inferiority process" faced by people of African descent and recognize their legitimate aspirations. Ms. Fanon Mendes said that coordination between Member States and civil society will help ensure that "this terrible legacy of history" is overcome. She further called for the historicization of the slave trade in order to realize a hypothetical and shared history and form an accurate sequence of racist construction sequences.

"If we want to question the political and social construction of race, including its role in the abolition of slavery, during this period, free men have no choice but to continue working on their former master's plantation. This is indispensable. Steps. Emerging from the painful past." She explained. She also emphasized that it is necessary to deconstruct all assumed racial myths by "eliminating" any factors that lead to inequality and structural discrimination. The UNICEF Goodwill Ambassador Harry Belafonte was another keynote speaker. He recalled the time he spent with the legendary African American actor Paul Robeson, who said that the artist is the guardian of the truth. The moral compass of mankind therefore, Mr. Belafonte went on to say that he tried to use art as a tool to unite the human family.

He went on to say that although the "strong alliance" of World War II was supposed to end fascism and intolerance, a serious flaw is that the Allies are equally guilty of racial oppression as Hitler." Races before and after the war for decades. Oppression, discrimination and intolerance mean that "most people of color know very little about people in the diaspora... our depth as people of African descent is not well known to each other. However, Mr. Belafonte emphasized that the United Nations is "a place to sit down and discuss cruel matters of racism and classicism", and he looks forward to the upcoming discussions and other speakers' speeches. And participants.

Finally, he emphasized that investigation and supervision agencies should have the power to deal with allegations of racial, and ethnic profiling, and make practical recommendations on policy changes, and called for effective supervision of the discretion of law enforcement personnel to reduce risks. However, it was not until the 1930s when Leon Trotsky used the adjectives "racist" and "racism" in his "History of the Russian Revolution" that France began to use these names. This kind of vocabulary, its cultural meaning is to make the traditionalist Slavs qualified to defend their own culture and national lifestyle.

Some people may not accept the truth about racism, and officials still have not used the necessary strategies to end this scourge. In Europe, racism is developing rapidly like other countries in the world. However, administrative procedures should prove that the measures taken are effective and can lead to overall success. But I noticed that the inefficiency of services is completely different from legal standards. The mobilization ability of racism victims is indeed very different: the most active people are likely to contribute to a strong realistic image of this phenomenon when they affect them, while the poorest people have more difficulty in entering public places. The media itself will hardly help provide an informed and explanatory image of the hatred or prejudice they suffer.

Again, statistics show that racist violence has increased. This fact proves that this expansion of violence is a completely different phenomenon. The police should be the protector of everyone, whether you are a citizen or a foreigner. In most cases, we realize that some police officers/women are hundred percent racists and they are doing work that hates black people. They will do everything they can to ensure that the victim's race and skin color are blamed. Sometimes I even ask myself, is racism not a disease? I don't see any reason for us to fight, discriminate, humiliate each other, it's just a matter of skin color.

Simplicity of Life

"Being a simple, optimistic, and strong person means that you value yourself rather than everything." We usually think of simplicity as giving up our external property and using only the necessities. Of course, this is a large part of it. But the journey, I am learning is not only external, but also internal. To get real abundance from normal things, one must start from the inside. Just as some people have accumulated something to create a false identity or pursue a fabulous state of happiness, it is also short-sighted to eliminate one's own possessions without inner truth. They have been disconnected.

Try to be someone you are not, and you will never be. Living a conscious journey of self-growth can lead to a fulfilling life. It works through your true self, living a simple life. It is good at simplicity. Self-simplicity becomes the clarity of your search for meaning. This is to remove unnecessary things. This is your most important discovery. Self-simplicity is the intersection of self-care. This is my favorite dress. Because of the simplicity of maintaining my state, I was able to eliminate unnecessary energy that would seep into my clothes. In the morning, I spent a few minutes sitting at the table with my family for breakfast before we went out. It can reduce my stress and anxiety throughout the day.

Since our mobile devices are the bridge that connects us to the world, this is also the key to keeping us out of today's life. After years of testing by pessimists, it is time to look in the mirror and change the way of behavior. Automatically, even your family will become closer and your attention will no longer be distracted. We play more, we have spontaneous dance parties, we listen to music and sing together, we read and read by ourselves, we spend quiet time together. To live not only for yourself, but also for those in need, you must share some love with them. Don't let your ego speak for you.

Your ego will spit out all the things you should do, not what you were doing at the time. It eliminates your own source of feed.

Most people don't like to get up in the morning because they have work. The unfortunate reality is that we spend a third of our time in the workplace. Be as good as everyone, just as you are.

Changing the way of thinking about working can enrich your life. It is no longer a balancing act between work and life, but life itself. got engaged. Remove yourself from gear-like behavior and inject your unique abilities into everything you do. It makes getting up in the morning much easier.

In the past, your daily goal was to work hard to get promoted, get a more prestigious title and a bigger salary. Since the implementation of self-care, office politics has become less attractive, the competition for the corporate ladder is no longer purposeful, and the prestigious title is now just words. This is the duty of some people. Focus on the changes that only you can do. The new meaning will appear immediately. It used to feel like you had to say "yes" to everything. This is what the road to success looks like. Usually, these promises and obligations that you agree will cause unnecessary pressure and friction in the relationship between your family, friends, and colleagues. Everything you do every day.

The ability to refuse provides space in my life, allowing you to focus on the things you cherish or own the most. This is not to participate in everything, but to involve yourself in the right things. Life lives between the moments we often pass in a hurry. It is in the car going to the daycare, standing in line with your son in the grocery store, reading to the children before going to bed, or cleaning the table with the family. This is part of everything in our lives, and we tend to hide ourselves. But these are simple memories that will be unforgettable in a lifetime. These are all experiences that write our stories and shape our lives. These simple things are important and have become the things we admire most.

Simple living encompasses a number of different voluntary practices to simplify one's lifestyle. Simple living may be characterized by individuals being satisfied with what they have rather than want. Although asceticism generally promotes living simply and refraining from luxury and indulgence, not all proponents of simple living are ascetics. Simple living is distinct from those living in forced poverty, as it is a voluntary lifestyle choice.

Adherents may choose simple living for a variety of personal reasons, such as spirituality, health, increase in quality time for family and friends, work life balance, personal taste, financial sustainability, frugality, sustainability or reducing stress. Simple living can also be a reaction to materialism and conspicuous consumption. Some cite socio-political goals aligned with the environmentalist, anti-consumerist or anti-war movements, including conservation, degrowth, deep ecology, and (anti-war).

Extravagance is often a portrayal of unsatisfactory life. When you simplify, you will get a life full of meaning, which is a life of living according to your own wishes. You have time and space to pursue your interests and create the life you truly desire. We often find true happiness in the simplest things.

Complex Inferiority

What experience does he have? Why did you decide this way? then? You cannot turn a natural behavior of the day into a supernatural phenomenon for no reason. Therefore, by analyzing the situation, it can be concluded that, according to the obvious point of view, this automatic change determines the victim's failure or disappointment, pain, and self-esteem. On a good day, someone decides to change from an honest person to a dishonest person, an annoying person, a criminal, etc. We cannot ignore the trauma that prevents us from becoming ourselves. It is easy to judge others, but getting yourself into trouble is a challenge. To talk about democracy, we must make it a reality based on theory and practice. In other words, apply its three basic EEE Who doesn't want to achieve it? This is everyone's wish. Have a better life and have everything that life needs.

Putting down one's feet, the fact that the lack of access to basic necessities is an anomaly and a major obstacle to see if the latter evolves in the environment, contempt, racism, ignorance, arrogance, and discrimination triumph every day. There is automatically a sign of inferiority complex. The truth we don't know; in the real situation in some countries, the voice of war has not stopped. The final solution can save many lives, among them desperate victims, abandoned by their country. No one chooses white, yellow or black.

It is quite simply the decision of two human beings, they

decide to spend a moment of relaxation of sex, pleasure, enjoyment. Subsequently, a child was born.

This can be two people of the same or different nationality who give birth to offspring of white, black, mixed race etc.

Should we condemn someone because of their race, nationality, skin color, economic means or religious orientation?

No! It would be unfair and absurd.

Who does not like money, luxury, nice clothes, nice car etc.? Everyone loves and wants to have it? If you've had the chance, and you're not one of the vulnerable, thank goodness!

Rather than making them feel uncomfortable, it is better to frame them and extend a helping hand to remind them that we are all brothers. Hospitals, nursing homes, close patients are hospitalized, and sick people can understand reality. The existence of every human on earth remains a real mystery.

In other words, a person is not superior to another view of his origin, and it is necessary to get rid of this myth in your mind. The patient in the hospital is very painful, because he is in a coma and cannot recognize himself, so he cannot take care of himself, he is automatically subconscious.

The identity of people in nature has been restored. Permanent improper use right.

Don't be fooled by anyone who tries to make a difference in your life. Life is good, it is simple. Most negative thoughts and discomfort exist mainly because we have made too many speculations about uncertainties and toxic substances. Because too many people lack self-confidence, there are all these fears and doubts. The important thing is to believe in yourself, don't be afraid to cross obstacles, and try your best to make the impossible possible. You must be careful not to do several things at the same time. It has become a normal phenomenon, and it is hoped that multiple operations can be performed at the same time. The results are usually bad.

Just because everyone is doing it does not mean that you have to comply with this constraint. Become the sole master of your own life and your own happiness. You can only live once. The day you stop breathing, life is over! Happiness is an inner pursuit, only you know what makes you happy. When there is a good atmosphere around, it is easier to face difficulties. The happier you are, the better your chances of improving relationships with relatives and strangers. Your goal should be the quality of the results, not the quantity. For some people, it is almost natural to make life more difficult. Indeed, interpersonal relationships have never been so simple. Simple life is the best choice, but sometimes it is complicated. Simpler!

Discrimination

If we explore the issue of discrimination when defining the ethnology of terms, we can understand the roots of racism. Ethnology: From discriminatory Latin to criminals, from the perspective of separation. In the social sphere, discrimination is the negative difference, isolation, and isolation between a person or a group of people and the larger whole. It consists in restricting the rights of certain people by imposing specific unfavorable treatment on certain people, and has no objective relationship with determining a larger whole. Whether it is voluntary or unconscious, discrimination undermines the equality of rights and opportunities, but it also undermines the equality of everyone's responsibilities. It is discrimination to separate others from others by treating them worse.

Many people are discriminated against because of their skin color. Every country in the world should be the first country to ensure respect for everyone's rights. Unfortunately, many people are victims of discrimination every day. In most cases, this is caused by the non-application of laws protecting human rights. By drawing on the tradition, according to the different groups of people, the particularity of specific groups of people and its governor usually tolerate the economy. Discrimination occurs in many forms and is not conducive to the treatment of another race. This is based on an illegal and unacceptable method.

In order for an act to constitute discrimination, it must

involve an illegal standard: race, religion, national or social origin, language, appearance, ancestry, gender, sexual orientation etc.

Discrimination can take many forms, starting with the deprivation of basic rights, such as migration, nationality and even freedom of speech, religion or sexual orientation... It may also bring unequal and unfavorable treatment to the public. The level of employment, housing or access to education and care. It was pointed out that during the economic crisis, discrimination against certain ethnic groups or communities has greatly increased, and there is an unfair responsibility for this situation.

In democratic countries, the law is one of the most effective means to combat all forms of discrimination. However, when discrimination is a common social habit, this struggle becomes more difficult. However, discrimination can also take indirect forms and become the basis for violations of other human rights, such as deprivation of liberty, cruel and degrading treatment, and crimes against humanity. Skin color, sexual minorities and ethnic minority women are still the main victims of this discrimination. Examples of discrimination:

1- A black woman was arrested and humiliated by the police for the order of an influential former white man.

2- Dark-skinned people are rejected by the university.

3- The foreigner is refused to participate in the job interview because of his nationality. Speaking of discrimination, one must also understand the strategy of equilibrium. This is actually a fantasy, contradicting the social state or the logic of identifiable social organizations in various places.

Every society experiences differentiation and social

discrimination. This structured organization is based on the use and distribution of wealth. Such discrimination will cause inconvenience between people.

Discrimination is the main obstacle to "live together". The automatic rejection of his public relations on the issue of superiority made him miserable and put him in an atmosphere of cruelty and hatred. If each of us practice this way of expression, then the world will become more meaningful:

"Everyone is born equally and respects the law."

1- Accept the rights of others.

2- Whatever your destiny, you are equal.

3- Black or white, Caribbean or British, we are all "human"

We should likewise salute each one of the individuals who have consistently declined a joint effort whatever its structure to bind together, embarrass or victimize his neighbor by the reality of not having an incredible economy, its strict direction and so on.

I might want to respect and salute numerous understudies who are survivors of bigoted segregation in school, college for the opposite lead of their instructors, individual understudies.

We must also congratulate all those who have always refused a collaboration whatever its form to unify, humiliate or discriminate against his neighbor by the fact of not having a powerful economy, its religious orientation etc.

I would like to honor and congratulate many students who are victims of racist discrimination in college, university for the contrary conduct of their teachers, fellow students.

At school, there are two types of discrimination: Direct or indirect discrimination. Discrimination in education is not very frequent and indirect discrimination systems are very difficult to spot. Therefore direct discrimination takes its form when, for example, a schoolboy or student automatically refuses to sit together because of his skin color. In conclusion, the concept of discrimination is not unanimous, moreover, some preferring to speak of inequalities, equity, equal opportunities or even the ethnicization of reports.

This long-standing subject should therefore be the subject of current research on the issue of discrimination in schools around the world. The teaching practices, the functioning of establishments and institutions, the question of living together at all levels: social, sexual, ethnic, etc. are important points to discuss while working to fight effectively against discrimination at school, university, work and in our surroundings.

Despite the publication in 1960 of the convention against discrimination in education. This convention reminds us that the principle of non-discrimination and the right of everyone to education are enshrined in the Universal Declaration of Human Rights.

In this text, the term discrimination includes any distinction, exclusion, limitation or preference which, based on race, color, sex, language, religion, political opinion, or any other opinion, national origin, has the object or effect of destroying or impairing equality treatment in education.

The prohibition of discrimination Article 14, despite the prohibition that does not prevent some people continue to ignore the texts prescribed by the Convention for the Protection of Human Rights and Fundamental Freedoms of 1950.

Opportunists are always looking for advantages of all kinds, they are often consider them mercenaries without borders.

Friendship by its definition, a reciprocal feeling of

affection or sympathy that is neither founded nor on kinship or sexual attraction.

A relationship of friendship is today defined as a lasting sympathy between two or more people with no physical or psychological attraction.

Friends are real supports making it possible to directly influence our moods, our happiness, to help us overcome trials, allowing us to laugh like never before to smile, to enjoy simple moments and sometimes support you in difficult times. The definition of friendship allows us to understand strengths and its importance.

Following the different meanings, it comes down to concluding that friendship is first and foremost an ally. If we are talking about friendship at work, at school, at university.

Once, I was sitting in a cafeteria, a black student was abandoned, humiliated alone others are not interested in the student simply because he is not white.

A language trouble could consequently be the justification the detachment yet this isn't the case they don't speak with an unfamiliar understudy for a racial inquiry, shading and so forth.

As though the last has carried out a wrongdoing, many are casualties of segregation as a result of their ethnicity, their dark skin tone. Be that as it may, the papers scarcely discuss it.

The most exceedingly terrible, his last figure that an understudy of dark tone doesn't have the limit of thinking the stakes of the bigotry question. We will at last need to place the issue of prejudice on the table to discover an answer to assist all men regardless.

The issue of bigotry has changed the attitude of numerous men and most of individuals casualties of prejudice end gravely. The myth remains and hard to adjust. Also, that consequently makes a vacuum in their framework mental. The antiquated logician Aristotle said: "Nature loathes a vacuum." That thing is dull and scentless.

A similar standard is busy working in our clairvoyant life. At the point when individuals begin to persuade us regarding our character by putting us down, the possibility of not tolerating this contention promptly rings a bell.

We give a valiant effort to defeat this negative power. Then again, any endeavor to relinquish our musings, perspectives and fantasies is bound to disappointment in light of the fact that the end of one makes a void in our everyday life.

Be bigoted on the appearance of being fulfilled, rich, having light hair, excellent green eyes, dim, and so on. This is pointless.

Dark cleaned men ought to likewise change their outlook not to consider white to be as their adversaries.

We can't change what is unchangeable, for instance the past, awful recollections state time yet we can change tomorrow to guarantee that servitude never happens again on the planet.

We are destined to live respectively in any event, when I know for some it is unthinkable on the grounds that the fantasy of predominance is typified in their psyche and their idea.

The historical backdrop of every individual's life demonstrates it; the historical backdrop of every country and its current circumstances demonstrate it.

Aristotle arrived at this resolution by taking note of that nature requests that all space be loaded up with something, in any event, when it appears to be difficult to a few.

In attempting to show an environment, a picture that is and never will be the best regardless of what you can offer, offer to turn it in any case acknowledge that it is unthinkable. You won't ever have the option to change what has been customized by the idea of the human body in general.

You need them to manage responsibilities that you would prefer not to do out of prevalence complex.

They will all need to utilize the demise of George Floyd to give another tone to the unseemly pictures drawn against individuals of color.

On interpersonal organizations, Internet clients, from the United States and somewhere else, are requesting "equity for George Floyd", another image of police viciousness against dark Americans.

"It's not simply an issue of prejudice" – disdain is going full bore, quarrels among highly contrasting individuals.

"It's a matter of brutality" – an old history dated for quite a long time in the event that we return on schedule to the state. This issue has not yet been settled.

The savagery of a police power in the picture of that of the entire of society, against a foundation of individual and institutional prejudice. The time has come to take care of this issue.

The subject of prejudice and savagery, "two significant issues".

The Issue of Racism

Wherever on the planet individuals are murdered every year by the police, as per computations blacks address almost twenty five percent of the people in question. "A fourth of individuals murdered by the police are blacks. It has consistently been in this way, as per factual information."
Published by Statista Research Department
Statista Inc. 3 World Trade Center 175 Greenwich Street; 36th Floor New York, NY 10007 United States.

Unfortunately, the trend of fatal police shootings across the United States appears to only increase, with a total of 1,096 civilians shot and killed in 2022, 225 of whom will be black. On January 25, 2023, there were 79 police shootings. In 2021 there were 1,048 fatal shootings. Additionally, black Americans had a far higher rate of police shooting deaths than any other race, at 5.9 per million population per year, between 2015 and January 2023.

Blacks are 2.5 occasions more probable than whites to be slaughtered by the police. The interracial inquiry is the object of any quarrel of prejudice and brutality. Two significant issues. A difficulty that could accordingly be tackled by the equipped specialists, this acknowledgment is significantly more significant than the time given to preparing in brain science or compromise.

This danger of continually being confronted with a

disappointed and furious lion's share.

Some cops who overstepped the law each time actually utilize self-preservation contentions. Mistakes of appreciation which, additionally, regularly permit the police to be delivered by the courts, on account of the summon of this theory. The cops associated with a few unlawful captures have never attempted, they are everywhere, while the casualties look for equity.

Racial Segregation in Government

We are seeing a "duplication of types of separation" A large number of bigoted conduct. In this way, while most segregating circumstances happen inside the system of progressive relations or with the organization manager, understudies, schoolchildren-educators, laborers, the reactions show an expansion in the issues between them.

Segregation that has nothing to do ... with affronts or abuses should likewise be rebuffed notwithstanding its structure, it is likewise called separation.

Truth be told, to separate is to disallow or restrict an individual's admittance to work, preparing or vocation improvement for reasons recommended by law. All things considered, no incredible exertion is made in forbidding the unfortunate conduct of sick intentioned people who are illegal and sworn not to keep the principles.

Maligning and affront are additionally disallowed by law. For instance, racial affront is an offense that is deserving of the Penal Code. Be that as it may, a lot more disregard the laws.

An inappropriate denied right is simply separation, anyway the casualty can demonstrate it from the second she has hints, unmistakable components of an all-around characterized circumstance.

Confronted with separation, still so continuous, present all over the place and a general absence of response from the people in question, it is significant in 2020 that the last take part in the counter bigoted battle.

The thought isn't to denounce, nor to deride the present circumstance, yet is to ensure that the organizations concerned comprehend the degree of this issue and battle the heaviness of bias.

To discuss segregation, there should be a boycott, a limitation on an individual's admittance to business, preparing or vocation improvement for reasons recommended by law.

Consequently there is a break in equity between two individuals who are in an indistinguishable circumstance, and treated contrastingly for precluded reasons.

Slander and affront are likewise denied by law. What's more, individuals couldn't care less about the results.

Racial put-downs, all things considered, embarrassing, offending somebody to the purpose of needing to surrender to one another is an offense which is deserving of the Penal Code.

Obviously, certain proportions of inside association at work taken by a progressive predominant, an administrator, a chief or a business can try not to hide an oppressive measure.

Forestall segregation and assurance equivalent common freedoms. The guidelines to be followed to advance the foundation of a non-unfair arrangement and lead in broad daylight and private capacities. On the program, key advances, for example, fabricating an unmistakable and solid message, both inside and remotely; make a common stock; a merged examination of issues and arrangements. A need if the entertainers need to secure counteraction and assurance long haul equity.

In spite of true information from true insights and logical investigations demonstrate the degree of segregation dependent on birthplace and its fundamental measurement in the public arena.

Individuals of unfamiliar starting point or saw as such are distraught in admittance to work or lodging and more presented to joblessness, instability, helpless lodging, police checks, chronic frailty and disparities school.

They are now and then spread in the homeroom. Segregation connected to racial and ethnic inception ought to hence pull in considerably more safeguards of rights and the specialists concerned. It would not be difficult to end bigotry not before we change the protection strategy. Most of individuals who guarantee to be advocates for survivors of bigotry are themselves bigots.

Race and Racism (Lies and Hypocrisy)

This bigoted inquiry, a story that doesn't trace all the way back to 2020.

The formula has been demonstrated since the Third Republic, turning into the brand name of conservative prejudice: assign the inner adversary, by assaulting laborers of public minorities (Roma, Arabs, blacks, Jews, whom the patriot philosophy assigns as an exogenous minority, barring them from the "public body"...) and outsiders.

This is the strategy manufactured by the Bourgeoisie and the patriot flows to battle the laborers' development (after the authors of Versailles of the Third Republic had squashed the town) since the 1870s. To this is added the tradition of provincial prejudice of this equivalent "republic" that some present to us as an image of shelter despite state bigotry.

We should dispose of untruths, and pietism. There are numerous who exploit the marvel of bigotry and feel great in this insufficient climate where one layer proclaims to have the force, the way in to this world.

They debilitate the estimation of men of shading, they see them essentially as articles, a story to be updated and changed.

Progression of bigoted discourse and methodology of division:

The bigot and xenophobic addresses of specific governments address a further advance in the freedom of bigoted discourse and in the system of division by designating a substitute.

In lower-pay areas, this has additionally brought about an increment in the presence and forcefulness of the police, and hefty judgment of the face.

However, on the off chance that we should go against this heightening, by getting sorted out fortitude even with state constraint and prejudice, we should likewise not fail to remember that this abusive and bigoted strategy doesn't date from today.

The lip service is then to get enthusiastic when the patriot talk exploits this smelling philosophical agreement around the possibility of "nation", making an interpretation of it right into it.

To this perplexity of the "country" that the bourgeoisie and the state wave to cause us to accept that their advantages are our own, we go against class fortitude, the regular battle against bigot and xenophobic approaches.

Confronted with the state and the bourgeoisie, we go against the need to on the whole form a populist, libertarian culture, breaking with private enterprise, patriotism and the state.

We should dispose of Hitler's approach, that Nazi prophet, who added to the advancement of bigotry and all of history is clarified by the battle forever, a cruel conflict where the solid beat the frail. The human races best outfitted essentially pound the mediocre races.

The Aryans, of which the Germans are the vanguard, have as their predetermination and mission to crush the races of "sub-men": negroes, mutts, Slavs and Jews. No ethical thought ought to obstruct this exertion in light of the fact that, for Hitler, the regard because of the other is just "obscenity of feebleness".

Thinking in opposition to the truth of life.

By analyzing the characters of Hitlerite characters, it amounts to pointing out that they are jealous people who stormed the property of the Jews and of the naive people of his time.

To monopolize the property of its last, the Hitlerites used all forms of terror by intimidating people who were not interested in war.

The Hitlerites and their leader Hitler, however, strengthened the racial system by highlighting the question of class, color that the settlers themselves were successful in the days of the colony.

A successful conceptual strategy, they conquered, convinced the extremely naive people who accepted the unacceptable.

Become a slave one day without having thought about it, an anecdote, an unforgettable anomaly, but the challenge was to wake up one fine day and say no to slavery.

The abolition of slavery something that did not please a large number of racist people who never wanted to see people of black color sit in the same place, row with them to eat together, to find accommodation etc.

The immaturity behavior brought about by the behavior of racists, French or German. We had, for our part, a feeling of this order vis-a-vis the actions of the militiamen, proud arms capable of the most naive childishness, like the most repulsive crimes.

Racists considered as immature people, still absurd, stupid, wicked, they proclaim to be the only masters, chiefs, governors of the past, they could have had adequate attitudes of the present moment.

Bigotry was imagined to exploit, to scare modest, guileless, genuine individuals, companions of harmony and of religion.

As per the story Gobineau is quick to articulate the predominance of the race, a whimsical dream who as indicated by his fantastical creative mind, having white skin tone, being fair all in all and starting point implies predominance.

An redoubtable fantasy dated for quite a long time and this one will stay connected in the personalities of each one of the individuals who have it since the base of their grandparents; their children and grandsons from one age to another.

They infer that to be dark is to be negro, unfortunate, reviled, disgrace.

Yet, the Aryan kind himself is in fancy with the truth of human existence, they think they are best positioned on the planet from a racial perspective, his shading white.

They had an ideal record against the underhanded individuals they controlled to cause them to acknowledge a wreck for reality - if, he is reasonable, with all the Aryan ethics, which would make him, as indicated by them, an unrivaled race.

Incidentally, it is simply the thought of race that is at issue. Allow us to acknowledge the definition given by E. Pittard, who believes competition to be the association of comparable people from guardians of a similar blood. Anthropologists are practically consistent in attesting that such gatherings are hard to track down. Unadulterated races don't exist.

They would prefer not to have bigoted discussions. They generally escape with the goal that reality doesn't come out. We cannot chain reality, it will ultimately uncover.

Since the beginning, we have seen that all conflicts have been advocated by champions, possibly they talk about self-preservation or they talk about battling the terrorists.

A need to shield against the "Terrorists"

From supported oppressions, the abused can't shield themselves against the barbarities.

What's more, on the off chance that we support Gobineau's realities, unmistakably prejudice spoke to bigots before and even today.

History, in any case, is loaded with bigoted discussions and there is a repercussion about the scourge. Wars have consistently looked to be advocated by the need to protect themselves against "brutes". The mistreatments needed to account for themselves by scorn of the abused. The "unrivaled races" didn't hang tight for the Comte de Gobineau and his "Exposition on the Inequality of Human Races" to develop the bias of race and find there the event for the vilest mistakes, the most brutal savagery.

Will we not, for instance, believe that among the Hindus, it was the possibility of race which managed the association of standings? The horrendous sentences, which are forced on the individuals who abuse the principles of the framework, express this thought that racial immaculateness should be saved no matter what. The Greeks have done everything, taken a stab at everything to forestall the association of various races and the Romans have duplicated laws planned to shield themselves from unfamiliar blood. To confront it, the Christian upheaval forfeited itself to declare the correspondence of every human race, from a similar stock, needed by a similar GOD.

It was anything but a simple battle, it took a ton of arm wrestling to arrive.

Stringently talking, indeed, we can concede racial sorts, controlled by certain anatomical or physiological characters. The height, the shade of the skin, the hair and the eyes: the cephalic record which prompts recognize dolichocephalic, brachycephalic, mesocephalic; the facial file, the nasal file, such countless characteristics that portray what has come to be known as a race. Without these trademark characteristics, everything being equal, we can't talk about a white race, yellow race, dark race. Besides, to recognize every individual his personality did not depend to a great extent on a distinguishing proof card at the beginning we can see it through his skin tone.

To these perceptions, to which anthropologists give, through estimations, a sort of numerical exactness, are added the characters which identify with specific properties of blood. It is without a doubt from their misjudged understanding that some discuss securing the "immaculateness" of blood: that of French blood or American blood or German blood. What's more, if these assumptions are smiling, it is very obvious that there are blood gatherings and that their investigation can intercede in the assurance of racial characters.

Anthropologists recognize races in Europe not without reason, they need to separate the class from the elites, the working class, the oppressed class. To regard Gobineau's norms and guarantee that its Gobineauniste standards are regarded exactly.

Gobineauniste laws have been applied wherever in Europe for instance in France, Germany and the United States to want to make part of the circle of incredible bigots.

Do we not realize that it was because of this silly and enthusiastic mission that Congress, in spite of Wilson's resistance, received the Johnson Act in 1924 to advance northern migration and cut off that of other "races?" »European?

Be that as it may, this "bigot" fierceness, which America is paying for now in a conflict against Hitler's Germany; in light of the fact that by shutting its entryways as South America did after it, as Australia was at that point doing, it released the craving for space among numerous people groups who are too inadequately given, nobody on the planet has it known to where it held onto the Germans. Governmental issues, a simple and troublesome game, which I think about like Football, Tennis, you are a star, powerful, famous player the entire city discusses however it's a disgrace that it differs from a limit of one to twenty years. "Genius is just exceptionally old."

Experience and naivety, pride and double dealing, aspiration and hopelessness have met up to make a spell on the possibility of race. The Germans persuaded themselves that they were the relatives of the unadulterated Aryans, that as such they needed to sanitize their race of non-Aryans first if they somehow happened to recapture their significance and force. The Jews, the extraordinary casualties of the Hitlerite's, can't until the present time clarify the astral pride, the aspiration, the objective of Hitler's destabilization which caused them much torment and pity.

Is it truly fundamental, not to show the unfeeling idiocy of this complexity of current realities of late history, yet to review that the German public can't guarantee more than some other, to the virtue of the race?

At the point when pseudo-ethnologists build up a way of thinking of the German race dependent on the supposed prevalence of the Aryan race. It's clever! Sadly, they have not understood until now that the Germans are a long way from being all Aryans or Nords, it can't be unadulterated blood. It's a blend.

The Aryan sort, reveals to us the anthropologist Henri

Valois, is tall; "The body is slim, with expansive shoulders and a tight pelvis... The skin, pinkish white, doesn't become earthy colored in the sun, it takes on a prepared block tone with the development of spots. The hair is fair or earthy colored, the eyes are blue or green. One would promptly say to the individuals who accept, on the purposeful publicity asserts, that the Germans are Aryans, they should simply glance around. At the point when Hitler's troopers support the cases of the "race of masters" with their knifes, their very variety perpetrates on them the most immediate and conclusive refusal. There are some among them who are "Nordic", yet there are other people who are real "High", and others "Dinaric" and still others "Eastern Europeans". "Obviously the combination of blood is in the race and in different races of the world. It is unreasonable to deny a particularly unmistakable truth.

At the point when William II, maybe prevailed upon by the speculations of Chamberlains and Ammon, supporters of Gobineau, needed to have an anthropological guide of the Reich drawn up, he understood that the racial attribute of Germany was variety and interbreeding. He surrendered his undertaking, almost certainly enlivened by the Vereinigung-Gobineau, which had made itself the proselytizer of the racial thoughts of Germany. It is said that the Nazis likewise had a somewhat comparative case.

The possibility of blood bunches having allured them, they needed to show that German Jews had a place with an unfamiliar gathering with "German blood". They rushed to perceive that every one of them were crossbreeds, as were most Germans themselves, and related either to the blood gatherings of the East or to the blood gatherings of Western Europe.

France, one of the nation's facilitating numerous evacuees,

ought not drive out nations of prejudice in the twenty first century. The racial thought may have taken less cost there than somewhere else, however France is on the counter Semitism rundown and some French individuals are worried about securing the "immaculateness of the race" from "metics". No place in Europe, notwithstanding, are such cases all the more clearly as opposed to the idea of things. The entire history of France is that of a nonstop assimilation of unfamiliar gatherings from the South, the East, the North-East, the South-East. Ligurians, Iberians, Celts, Germans, Latins and Greeks chose its dirt, without checking these men who came from wherever who steadily joined themselves into the number of inhabitants in the country. France was the mixture wherein races from everywhere Europe were amalgamated; it is its amicable kaleidoscope. As indicated by Henri Valois, through his work Chez Nous, of (1943) "the presence of four extraordinary races: the Nordic race, the Lorraine race, the Alpine race, and the Mediterranean race".

He adds relatives of the old race of the Polished Stone Age and a few delegates of three races whose typical territory is extra-European: Armenoid, Southeast and Indo-Afghan.

He rushes to notice, besides, that "every one of these races are pretty much blended, so no locale is the restrictive seat of one". "Subsequently, he finishes up, France, anyway homogeneous, it very well might be as far as its development and its attitude is from an anthropological perspective, a mosaic of races". It is its social qualities that give it its solidarity, it isn't its racial attributes: it is, in a real sense, an ethnic gathering, it's anything but a racial gathering. He ought to comprehend that France is looking for giving another positive picture in opposition to the harsh memory of the times of the state. For another French history, the gathering of a wide range of race on the French region is a commitment or a need.

This racial inquiry has made such an extensive amount a mix everywhere on the world, particularly in Europe, it is a need to settle this undertaking which inconveniences the world and places men overall in a shower of disarray without having the option to wipe their countenances.

Gobineau was of his character, a cruel man, he looked for no matter what to persuade those whom they accepted feeble to acknowledge that nature had a place with him.

Any person would have jumped at the chance to have a cheerful life, satisfied to have all he requires to live.

All the time, it is an extra essentialness that the subjects that rise up out of it acquire. Hybridization is the standard of a perpetual re-establishment of the strength of people groups, as of people.

It isn't, as Gobineau accepted, the reason for all degeneration. The climate and history have another temperance. Furthermore, maybe one can trust that the people groups who, for the sake of the race, have done the most damage to mankind, have perpetrated the most wrongdoings against it, are probably going to change.

They should be freed of the racial persona, as it is important to battle all over the place and consistently the purported anthropological contentions which are just bogus science or criminal guises.

Prejudice is a social relationship that comes to fruition in a huge number of circumstances: activities, relationship games and social portrayals are for the most part measurements to be gotten a handle on to set up a spectrography of bigotry.

The cartoon of Christiane Taubira which showed up in the

first page of the paper Minutes, hence, frames part of a base of portrayals connected to the animality of "blacks". In this, it echoes the "monkey cries" that accentuate certain football matches (Bodinas, Robène and Héas, 2008).

This since she was the French Minister of Justice the way that she is dark, she ought not be. For the bigots of his time it was a mistake, a disgrace for France. They did everything to threaten him. Is it typical for this bizard conduct of men of letters?

The expressions of those engaged with public activity address an advantaged point of approach for getting a handle on the rationale hidden these articulations: from one viewpoint, it reveals insight into the manner by which people decipher lived circumstances while uncovering, then again, portions of the experience of oppressed people.

Contemporary symbols have another feature of the expression "race", prejudice and racialization is characterized in a setting explicit to contemporary France. For certain examiners, they comprehend that bigotry can likewise meddle in a design set apart by relations of mastery. The remarks of more youthful people, the characteristics of a dismissal not, at this point fixated on the possibility of race, yet on culture, Muslim religion, ethnicity and so forth.

Bigoted discourse proceeds to increment and casualties are concerned, they are looking for equity however those mindful are not very spurred in 2020.

The reference to ethnic classes gives a face to the disdain instigated by the experience of trickiness by highlighting substitutes.

Traditional prejudice depends on an origination of races as unmistakable and profoundly inconsistent organic elements, both actually and mentally. A malevolent assessment for the individuals who accept this to be genuine, they are mixed up like Mr. Trump.

Would it be advisable for it to have the prejudice topic? This subject should anyway pull out from vocabularies, word references and guarantee that it is never followed again. From that day on, the racial mysterious freedom will end consequently.

"Race" is as yet not a significant issue today, a verifiable, inexplicit complicit referential for people uncovered, during their childhood, to racialist speculations, you need to restart history, update your journals to figure out it to their challenges.

On the off chance that it has been logically demonstrated that races don't exist hereditarily and that we as a whole come from African progenitors, prejudice is verification actually.

Obviously there is a connection between mankind and bigotry, in addition, talking about prejudice is a token of the race. The differentiation between race as a natural idea and race as friendly constructivism which can be characterized as "a sign or a bunch of signs by which a gathering, a collectivity, a human entire is recognized, in specific settings exact narratives, this socially developed appearance changing as per the social orders, the occasions and furthermore the mindset of man as a rule."

To characterize the word race, history has consistently had the effect between race, nationality, cultural cause. Race (as a social build) has, notwithstanding, become generally free of the work completed on the natural grouping of individuals which has shown that the idea of human race isn't pertinent to portray the diverse geological subgroups of the species. human.

This end is, notwithstanding, challenged by A.W.F.

Edwards who, in his article Human Genetic Diversity: Lewontin's Error (2003), reprimands the contention, introduced in 1972 by Richard C. Lewontin. The Apportionment of Human Diversity contending that the division of humankind in races is systematically invalid.

The current logical agreement dismisses the presence of natural contentions that could legitimize the thought of race, consigned to a discretionary portrayal as per morphological, ethno-social, social or political measures. This independence is completely showed since the second fifty percent of the twentieth century when the impacts of the bigoted discernment framework have continued notwithstanding less regular use, and in spite of the dismissal of the idea of race by mainstream researchers. Ssus of African precursors, prejudice is no less present – it is even on the ascent Essay on the imbalance of human races is a work by the Frenchman Joseph Arthur de Gobineau distributed in 1853 and pointed toward building up the presence of races and the contrasts between them. The book will be one of the establishments of the bigoted philosophies of the century.

The perceptual system of prejudice can be separated into a few legitimate activities: Focusing, aggregation, essentialization and impediment, hierachization.

As to the concentration with regards to racism, is all that has to do with the pigmentation, the dark skin tone, the fuzzy hair, the way of life, the style of the person that permits him to stick out or explain its position, limit, area, class and so on.

Inside and out, bigotry partners actual qualities with good and social attributes. What places the casualties in an air of disquiet, a few people are impacted by others in the end they push them to change their ethnicity lamentably this doesn't transform anything since the skin tone doesn't change.

According to the bigot, "man goes before his demonstrations". On the off chance that the focal point of the bigoted look makes the objective body more noticeable than the others, it in this way likewise wipes out independence behind the overall class of race.

The bigoted considers the properties connected to a gathering as perpetual and contagious, regularly organically. The bigoted look is an action of arrangement and conclusion of the gathering on itself.

To contact the subliminal of the helpless, bigots regularly use proclamations to legitimize themselves.

The sentence "Blacks eat quick" consequently establishes a bigoted assertion in spite of its ameliorative appearance.

Bigoted talk can summon the actual predominance of the objective gatherings just as the energy or arousing quality of blacks to underline by contrast their scholarly inadequacy.

Be that as it may, much more, past the positive or negative substance of bigoted generalizations, the movement of classification, aggregation and limit of the person to biased properties isn't in itself a non-partisan action according to the perspective of qualities.

Antiquarians and ethnologists differ on the topic of the beginning of bigotry; two primary originations are gone against regarding this matter. The principal thinks about that prejudice is a side-effect of European free enterprise, connected to imperialism. The second is that various types of prejudice have succeeded each other from the beginning of time in Europe, and have done as such since Antiquity.

Since the second fifty percent of the twentieth century,

there has existed among history specialists a generally expansive agreement that the utilization of the thought of prejudice in classical times is a chronological error. To be sure, all old and crude social orders are, from our contemporary perspective, bigot and xenophobic social orders.

The Ancient Greeks recognize the people groups of Hellas from different people groups they call brutes. Practically any remaining antiquated people groups had similar double portrayal of the world in two races, related people groups, and unfamiliar or foe people groups; this resistance between two aggregates is the thing that characterizes the political area and the law of countries. A rationale which can't be demonstrated in all principles yet without a doubt in a couple of uncommon cases.

The utilization of the expression "race" as an indispensable equivalent word for individuals/ethnicity proceeded until the finish of the nineteenth century. Hence, the scholarly works of Jules Verne have large amounts of cliché recipes, for example, "the Germans, a productive and coordinated race", "the French, a heartfelt and heroic race" or "the Americans, an ambitious and dynamic race", even in discussions between old buddies of various starting points, without the smallest negative expectation in the utilization of the word. However, to talk about Africans, Caribbeans he would have changed the tone without a second thought briefly in spite of we as a whole realize that flawlessness doesn't exist.

The constructions of family relationship, in this way the inquiries of race, are consistently principal and establishing in the portrayal that old or crude people groups have of themselves and of different people groups. The entire arrangement of commitment and social fortitude of old or crude social orders depends on having a place with the family bunch, and to the more prominent or lesser closeness of connection.

Many white hued races coexist with one another with regards to their inclinations, they join for the last triumph something that I appreciate and I need to salute them for this association which for quite a long time has had them made dependable and renowned and so on.

Also, some venture to such an extreme as to affirm that the distinction exists between a dark and a white from an authoritative perspective the white man is more mindful than the person of color.

This is the reason, the further we go ever, the more we notice that the people groups who are customarily travelers or make a state, keep on wedding in the portion of the genome from which they are isolates, and not in individuals among whom they live.

Regarding the guidelines set up to oversee migration, it isn't so natural for an outsider to join with an occupant of this region. The standards and rules should be followed exactly.

A large number of them experience the ill effects of standards at times considered as innovation to go against relations between outsiders.

It ought to be noticed that at these occasions, these principles concern movement which isn't done exclusively, however with respect to the Phoenician, Greek or Carthaginian provinces, by complete gatherings equipped for reproducing somewhere else another indistinguishable and shut society.

Inquiries of war and harmony between clans or people groups start with refusals or breaks of marital unions, and end with collusions, or chains of coalitions, between heredities of bosses, and from that point the chance of relationship and union between the wide range of various families. Indicate that these remedies are forced on gatherings, yet not on disengaged people or disaffiliated families.

By stressing the scriptural story starts again the historical backdrop of Humanity after the flood, with the three children of Noah, Shem, Cham, and Japhet, from whom drop the three genealogies that occupy the shores of the Mediterranean. The Table of Peoples of Genesis gives, with the relatives of these three siblings, the genealogical inception of the multitude of people groups of the Earth which are introduced both as genealogically unmistakable people groups, and simultaneously related. This last quality, which reviews the uniqueness of the human realm, monogenism, is an inventiveness that isn't found in numerous crude people groups who hold the name of man, dismissing the others in the creature world, natives.

The origination as indicated by which the utilization of the idea of prejudice in Antiquity is an erroneous date, is raised doubt about by crafted by the student of history Benjamin Isaac who proposes the thought of "proto-bigotry" crossing Greek and afterward Roman Antiquity , an idea that is now important for a "conceptualized prejudice, in view of a contention of a logical perspective which is proposed to be decisive."

Proto-bigoted idea, which will clearly develop throughout the long term and the movements of focuses of impact and force, is based, as indicated by the student of history, on two speculations which won't be addressed definitely: from one perspective, following the composition on a pretense, water, places dating from the fifth century BC. Promotion and ascribed to Hippocrates, a deterministic order of human gatherings dependent on geographic territory which would characterize "unchangeable aggregate character qualities", in a plan which rapidly actuates a progression of people groups.

Everybody has a character or trademark which depends on their beginning, identity, nationality, culture and customs.

The logician Christian Delacampagne sees, as far as concerns him, in the agnostic disposition - Egyptian, Greek then Roman - towards the Jews and in the parcel between free men from one viewpoint, ladies, youngsters and slaves on different, "characterizations natural, bigoted sort.": Christian Delacampagne.

Book Reference: "A History of Racism" by Christian Delacampagne.

Translated from French by Ursula Vones-Liebenstein. De la Campagne covers the main historical stages of racism since ancient times. From medieval anti-Semitism as a deadly precursor to modern racial fanaticism to the era of colonial conquest. Now the victims are Indians and blacks in America. The delusion of a white or Germanic "master race" was intended to provide an ideological "justification" for National Socialism to massacre millions of Jews, Sinti and Roma. De la Campagne strongly condemned racism in Europe today, as well as racist-motivated genocide in many parts of the world.

According to Delacampagne, the idea that conversion absolves the Jew then fades away from the belief that Jewishness is a hereditary and intangible condition. This movement does not spare other categories of the population. Its most convincing manifestation is the gradual establishment from 1449 of a system of certificate of purity of blood (Limpieza de sangre) in the Iberian Peninsula to gain access to certain corporations or to be admitted to universities or orders. This movement, which results in the decree of the Alhambra of 1492, concerns four specific groups: the Jews, the converted Muslims, the penitentiaries of the Inquisition and the cagots, that is to say the presumed descendants of lepers. .

Delacampagne mentions the segregation which affects this last category of population as a major stage in the constitution of modern racism. According to him, this is the first time that the discrimination of a social group in the fourteenth century received a justification based on the conclusions of science. Surgeons, such as Ambroise Paré, indeed lend their support to the idea that cagots, presumed descendants of lepers, continue to carry leprosy although they do not show any external signs. Several studies have highlighted the existence of attitudes that their authors consider racist in societies outside the European cultural area. In Japan, the hereditary transmission of belonging to the Burakumin caste until the beginning of the year may have been the product of a symbolic construction of a racist type. The work carried out by historian Bernard Lewis on the representations developed by Muslim civilization with regard to other human beings concludes on the existence of a perceptual system that he qualifies as racist, in particular with regard to black populations. .

In the Middle Ages, the racism of Arabs against blacks, in particular non-Muslim blacks, based on the myth of the curse of Cham, the father of Canaan, pronounced by Noah, served as a pretext for the slave trade and slavery, which, according to them, applied to blacks, descendants of Cham who had seen Noah naked during his drunkenness. Blacks were therefore considered "inferior" and "doomed" to slavery. Several Arab authors compared them to animals. I cannot understand such behavior, the Arabs are of Egyptian origin and for those who know the history, they know very well that the Arabs are of

African origin. Why hate black people to compare them to animals, I am convinced there is a mystery, a hidden secret.

The poet Al-Mutanabbi despised the Egyptian governor Abu al-Misk Kafur in the tenth century because of the color of his skin. The Arabic word aabd (pl.aabid) which meant slave became from the seventh century more or less synonymous with "Noir", taking a similar meaning to the term "negro" in the French language of the twentieth century. As for the Arabic word zanj, it pejoratively designated blacks, with an official racial connotation that can be found in racialist texts and speeches. These racist judgments were recurrent in the works of historians and Arab geographers: thus, Ibn Khaldun was able to write in the fourteenth century: "The only peoples to truly accept slavery without hope of return are the negroes, by reason of a degree inferior of humanity, their place being closer to the stage of the animal."

At the same time, the Egyptian scholar Al-Abshibi wrote: "When the Negro is hungry, he steals and when he is full, he fornicates". An absurd and insignificant judgment that racists today still use to discredit all people of black color.

The land having a place with men, as a reasonable principle, there ought to be no man who professes to be the dominator of another man or the controller of the last mentioned. What's more, see to kidnap it until it turns into his private or individual article. A demonstration of sadness and against vote based which should at this point don't be rehashed for the admiration of majority rule government.

The different creators who think about prejudice as an explicitness of European advancement consent to feature the blend of three components in the beginning of this new disposition.

The advancement of present day science. It initiates an arrangement of essentialist view of otherness and an arrangement of avocation for bigoted conduct which depends on logically imagined hypotheses of race.

The advancement of against Christian free-thought which goes against the monogenism upheld by the Catholic Church.

European extension which started in the fifteenth century. It includes the foundation of a financial and social arrangement of subjugation, and focused on the states; simultaneously, it is joined by the advancement of a frontier mentality towards non-European populaces which is slowly entering the city.

The hour of the province every one of the slaves needed to bow to the sets of their lords regardless of what they didn't care for, a constrained renunciation which was difficult to beat a bygone era hard to dispose of a hook mare which is by and by a lived reality.

The topic of the anteriority or the successors of prejudice to the advancement of subjugation in the European states is as yet the subject of much discussion today.

Agreement is arising, nonetheless, about the pretended by the improvement of bondage in solidifying and spreading racial mentalities. Frontier subjection is surely growing, strangely, when humanism, the way of thinking of the Enlightenment (reasoning) and the hypothesis of regular law in Europe ought to sensibly prompt its judgment.

Prejudice in logical inconsistency with the standards and this inconsistency won't be long in being seen by a decent number of spectators who consider this marvel as a structure concocted to abuse the assets of blacks.

The solitary cunning making it conceivable to deny certain populaces the advantage of essential rights perceived to man in everyday comprises in having confidence in the presence of an order between the races. Anyway enemies of bigots see the matter from an aspect of their arrangement, assessment.

As per American antiquarian Isaac Saney, "Recorded archives validate the overall shortfall of general racial bias and ideas of racial prevalence and mediocrity before the rise of the overseas slave exchange."

In the event that the ideas of otherness and predominance existed, they did not depend on a racialized vision of the world.

Eventually the advancement of bondage and current science firmly connected in the development of present day prejudice.

The classification of "noso-politics" meets all requirements for the logician Elsa Dorlin the utilization of the classes of "sound" and "unfortunate" by the clinical talk applied first to ladies, at that point to slaves.

While the whites, considered "normally" unrivaled by doctors, are characterized as the norm of well-being, the personality of blacks is by contrast announced "obsessive"; it is the transporter of explicit infections, which just accommodation to the work system forced by the settlers can constrict, however hard to fix, as they appear to be characteristically connected to its inclination. Thinking of an untraceable nature.

Concerning the others, Christians will legitimize their abuse by perusing the Bible: they have three shades of skin, white, yellow and dark, which would come from the three children of Noah, Shem, predecessor of the Semites, Japhet, progenitor of the European people groups and Cham the reviled, precursor of the Africans. It is from Europe, the support of bigotry, that all that will disappear.

Government and colonization are annihilating the Indians

of Latin America: seen as savages, even barbarians, they are fiercely subjugated, simultaneously as proselytized, which isn't without logical inconsistency. Las Casas reviewed to no end during the Valladolid debate of 1550 that they were men, that the Pope and Emperor Charles V went against subjection, oppression and the slaughters proceeded. Arising free enterprise required gold, land, work and exchange openings.

Spectators named the twentieth century, the hundred years of the most exceedingly awful, the hundred years of battles described by the record of cruelty. This is the hundred years of slaughters, of mechanical eradication: the annihilation of 1,000,000 Armenians, arranged and denied by the Turkish express; the 6,000,000 Jews killed by the Nazis, not including the Gypsies; nearer to us, 1,000,000 Tutsis killed in 100 days by the Hutus.

Perverted individuals of the time continued in the strides, the ways of their pioneers to forfeit a populace of good individuals, of the guiltless. Numerous grievous and abhorrent wrongdoings were recorded in the entry of his soldiers of fortune, hunger for influence, cash, the property of others.

Simultaneously, designed negationism which advances exemption: the decimation of the Armenians will fill in as a model for Hitler.

Others practice unfair and bigoted approaches: And we see today in Europe in equitable states, the resurrection of extreme right gatherings with a pretty much carefully bigoted segment, which take up the methodology of the substitute around the subject of migration. The topic of movement which is until date uncertain and we had seen and heard regular demonstrations of prejudice. Over and over, bigots are at the center of attention, in the migration issue they pick who ought to or can move to their region by changing over the Dublin guidelines into their own predominant law.

The twentieth century was that of the battle against bigotry. It was an event for the uprising of the nations of the world generally influenced by the scourge, including Africa. A difficult that sets aside effort to determine. Obviously there is not really any will of the specialists to tackle this issue.

Current realities: the chain of importance at the help of force. It was with the three-sided slave exchange that private enterprise had its most noteworthy achievement. The complete figure would be eleven million Africans ousted by Europeans to America, purchased and sold as slaves, 1,000,000 of whom kicked the bucket adrift. The slave exchange was denied in France in 1815, subjugation nullified in 1848. In any case, until - there the scorn for blacks and the lack of concern of the elites - Voltaire himself was enhanced there are with the end goal that the exchange and the misuse of individuals, till the very end, succeed, to the point that one can discuss a genuine destruction.

Africa comes out damaged, and America, where interbreeding is unavoidable, organized until now by the development of a racial order, with disdain in course, as per the shade of the skin. We can see that it is as yet about influence and cash, and that has not changed from that point forward.

Montesquieu composed with as much incongruity as exactness: "The people groups of Europe having killed those of America, they needed to subjugate those of Africa, to utilize them to clear such a lot of land." Rousseau showed that the wellspring of disparities was in the social, in property, and not in nature.

Lamentably our dear Enlightenment, in the hundred years of progress in information and the creation of the beliefs of equity and opportunity, made the way for an as yet unclear irritation of what might later be called prejudice: naturalists, as Buffon and Linnaeus, embrace to arrange creatures and plants by species and by race.

Voltaire can express: "The race of negroes is a types of men not the same as our own as the race of spaniels is greyhounds. Perilous open entryway: from scientific classification, we will change the order from certainty to hypothesis."

By getting autonomous on January 1, 1804, Haiti, the previous French settlement of Santo Domingo, procured a solid emblematic status. First conflict lost by a European armed force against extra-European agitators for a very long while, the principal fruitful subservient revolt in present day history, the world's sans first dark republic. Here is the thing that the Haitian progressives achieved between the Bois Caïman function of August 14, 1791 and the day of the announcement of autonomy.

The state of Santo Domingo, chosen the western piece of the island of Hispaniola (the eastern part being a Spanish settlement), was established in 1627. Initially populated by Arawak Indians, the socioeconomics of the island will be immediately changed. In fact, from the beginning of the European presence, by dint of illnesses and slaughters executed by the Spaniards, the populace went from 1.6 million to 60,000 somewhere in the range of 1492 and 1507. Europeans in this island, the financial advancement of the island will be finished by bringing in dark slaves, a training utilized by both the Spanish and the French.

Santo Domingo becomes for France its most prosperous state, on account of the creation of sugar and espresso, of which Santo Domingo gives half of the world creations during the eighteenth century. However, the segment and political circumstance there is perplexing.

While slaves, imported in enormous numbers all through the eighteenth century, wound up comprising the significant piece of the populace (around 400,000 slaves for 450,000 occupants just before the French Revolution), white society itself was crossed by pressures, between the "Grands Blancs" (aristocrats and common who have become huge landowners) and the "Petits Blancs" (representatives, laborers, little merchants, and so on) Added to this is the presence of "free ethnic minorities" (free mulattoes and liberated blacks) yet whose legitimate fairness is indeed not perceived by white pioneers.

The Haitian Slave Revolution, the battles for the nullification of bondage, against imperialism, against bigotry and invulnerability have stirred hearts and here and there changed strategies.

Haiti, a country with an incredible history, an extraordinary image which at long last settled on subjugation and to dispose of this awful "Karma" they revolted one day and they will bring forth the Haitian unrest.

However, two reasons will turn the circumstance around once more:

- Now drove by the savage General Rochambeau, the French armed force is occupied with ridiculous maltreatments.

- The previous dark slaves and the mulattoes understand that the genuine goal of the campaign is the restoration of subjugation (which was restored in Guadeloupe in the fall of 1802).

While the Toussaint Louverture camp was isolated (Dessalines had joined France in mid-1802 in the wake of being crushed by Leclerc's military, and had even partaken in the capture of Toussaint Louverture) and that of the mulattoes (Pétion, Boyer) had gotten back to Saint-Domingue on the side of the French armed force, these two camps joined together and rebelled against France.

Dessalines turned into the officer of the agitators. On November 18, 1803, the French armed force was crushed at Vertières and Rochambeau needed to give up all the while. This is the finish of the Santo Domingo endeavor, whose human cost is substantial.

It set up Haiti in 1804 as the principal free republic on the planet, succeeding the French settlement of Saint-Domingue.

On January 1, 1804, the settlement of Santo Domingo stopped to exist. It offers route to another state: Haiti (from the name utilized by the Arawaks to assign their island: Ayiti). Dessalines announced himself lead representative (at that point head) and had a large portion of the white populace slaughtered in the months that followed (around 5,000 casualties), for dread that they would approach unfamiliar forces to come and break the incipient Republic.

France will perceive the freedom of Haiti in 1825 through the voice of King Charles X. The new nation will consequently need to pay remuneration of 90 million gold francs, which will be settled completely somewhere in the range of 1825 and 1883. A solicitation or the law, each person conceived free and ought not be held prisoner by gatherings of men or people and see to request a tremendous entirety to be a liberated individual. In the event that we investigate the historical backdrop of Haiti, a solid, bold country, a country in the end that France should consider reimbursing and fulfilling.

Global law specialists have conveyed solid messages to the

specialists communicating their discontent and legal scholars have likewise made weapons against bigotry, for instance proclaiming decimation imprescriptible and its forswearing a wrongdoing.

Since the Universal Declaration of Human Rights, which starts by conjuring "the inborn poise of all individuals from the human family", prior to setting down as standards balance of rights, the preclusion of racial separation and subjection, the United Nations and UNESCO have delivered numerous apparatuses against bigotry and segregation: the Declaration on the Elimination of All Forms of Racial Discrimination (UN, 1963), the Declaration on Race and Racial Prejudice (UN, 1978), which upheld the execution of approaches to battle bigotry and imbalances, and so on.

We will zero in on the Expert Declaration on Race Questions (UNESCO, July 20, 1950), coming about because of a world program to battle prejudice.

It avowed the solidarity of the human species, relative of Homo sapiens, invested with a lot more grounded likenesses than contrasts, with as a typical trademark, "its personnel to learn and its pliancy"; she denied any association between the natural and the psychological or the social, and finished up: "truly, 'race' is less an organic marvel than a social legend. Among the eight signatories was Claude Lévi-Strauss, who was to distribute a significant book, Race and History, in 1952.

He inspires the key blunder of Gobineau and his supporters: to have connected the organic and the social, of which the incalculable varieties, continually moving, have no connection to the shade of the skin. From one viewpoint there is the organic and physiological advancement of human bodies, on the other a limitless number of societies connected to given social orders, and whose alliance produces what he calls "world development."

Notwithstanding these battles, today we see the most noticeably terrible renewed: hostile to Semitism, against Arab prejudice, the chase for Roma, covered up or not behind ideological groups that discuss France as a "white race" and "bacterial migration", getting back to the language of authentic bigots. Prejudice is a distortion, conjectured by nineteenth-century scientism; hostile to bigotry, then again, depends on logical information or isn't the topic of conversation.

The words: from "race" to "prejudice" "Race" comes from the Italian razza, a type of individuals, or from the low-Latin proportion, types of creatures or organic products, apheresis of generation, family, plunge, and species. The race is most importantly the heredity, the family, and accordingly, in the feeling of the Bible, the human species, which plunges from Adam and Eve: for a Christian mankind is a solitary family or should it be.

We utilize "race" from the eighteenth century for creatures, assigning an organically steady assortment inside similar species: the ox-like species checks the Norman race, the canine species tallies the spaniels and the greyhounds , and so on.

Applied to people, the word is practically difficult to characterize; we presently realize that eighty five percent of the hereditary legacy is regular to the entirety of mankind, which also is considerably more portable, and the sky is the limit from there is a ton of contention about the sources of humankind: the fundamental discussion in the eighteenth, nineteenth century happens between monogenists, similar to the savants Kant and Herder, and polygenists, similar to Voltaire, around this inquiry;

let us recollect that Christianity is hypothetically monogenist. At that point comes determinism, which advances the possibility of the interface between soil, environment, food, and human life systems just as mores and society; at that point Darwin's hypotheses of development (On the Origin of Species, 1859).

He is a monogenist, however the possibility of natural choice makes him believe that a few "races" are "less developed" than others. Herbert Spencer takes this evolutionism and applies it to the social, and articulates as the law of history the reformist triumph of the "fittest". From that point develops the dread that the lower races will beat the higher races, that their blood will be harmed and that there is racial degeneration.

It was a Frenchman, Count Arthur de Gobineau (1816-1882), who was additionally a fair author and scholar, who was quick to conjecture the progressive system of races—he didn't characterize race, placed as self-evident—and the legend of an alternate blood, in his Essay on the Inequality of Human Races, in 1855. From one perspective, he groups the races: white, savvy, dark, delicate and savage, yellow, innovative. The predominant race is obviously the white, itself partitioned into Caucasians (German and Frankish Aryans, Celts and Slavs) and Semites. Suppose in passing that he's not enemy of Jewish. Then again, he has faith in natural determinism and connections the organic to the social.

The law of the historical backdrop of human advancements is the passing of the white race since its blood should definitely be sullied with that of others. Truth be told, he stretches out to the historical backdrop of men a completely distinguished and biologized vision of respectable legacy. Right now, Gobineau's outcries have no impact.

Then again, he has a reverberating successors, particularly in Germany with Houston Stewart Chamberlain, future researcher of Hitler. Since it is with Gobineau that we move from racial speculation to bigoted reasoning. Science will work together, through humanities and Broca's anthropometry, phrenology, craniology ... The move is lethal: it permits the researcher theorization of what takes this new name of "prejudice" and which will attack history, humanities and legislative issues.

Out of dread and contempt of the other, we make an instrument of government and misuse that will be utilized past envisioning. With two variations: liberal, which supports imperialism, or selective breeding, which will prompt extradition and killing. Three comments in passing: this fantasy of blood isn't completely new. Limpieza de sangre, "immaculateness of blood", is an idea that has created in Spain and Portugal.

From the finish of the fifteenth century to assign "genuine Christians", without Jewish or Moorish heritage, who, rather than constrained believers, consistently dubious, had just access and right to significant capacities; and the general thought of nobility depends on legacy and organic transmission through blood, "nobility".

Then again, if "bigotry" emerges simultaneously as its hypothesis, we have seen that bigoted practices originate before their arrangement. At long last, past the endless varieties of originations of race, connected to the land for Michelet, to the climate for Taine, to language and culture for Renan, apparently the general concept of race is acknowledged by all peers, even reformist ones, and will prompt a general and enduring agreement for expansionism, for the sake of the humanizing mission of France.

Also, we go, as a family, to consider human examples in the zoos of the Universal and Colonial presentations: this is the means by which bigotry turns out to be essential for famous mores. In France in the nineteenth century, it was first around the Jews that bigotry made its fortune. The explanation is that since the Revolution, they have been liberated: they have obtained citizenship and equivalent rights and some of them are very few, the larger part stays dark and helpless hang out in the actual heart of society, getting in from the July government of incredible investors, extraordinary industrialists, even well-known craftsmen.

Before long it is on the extreme right that:

1) against Judaism transforms into hostile to Semitism. Hostile to Judaism held transformation as an answer for deleting the Jews; against Semitism keeps up that nothing eradicates their race;

2) hostile to Semitism becomes around 1880-1890 a genuine political, against vote-based program, based on connivance which by definition has the benefit of managing with no evidence: a Jewish global, connected to the Freemasons, would look to hold onto Europe and human advancement; they are all over the places, residents and white, imperceptible hard to follow them, they are extremely watchful.

The trademark is to dispose of the Jews, an authentic irresistible infection which clarifies all that isn't right: the Prussian triumph and the deficiency of Alsace-Lorraine, the monetary emergency, the monetary accidents and the shortcomings of the Republic. Edouard Drumont, with La France juive 1886, turned into an energetic missionary of this program and soon the spirit of the counter Semitic mission against Dreyfus. Bigotry is rediscovering the old substitute technique, however now it is transforming it into an administration program.

There have been a few instances of common freedoms infringement and fundamental racial segregation in the United States during the battle against the COVID-19 pandemic. These cases were accounted for at the forty fifth meeting of the United Nations Human Rights Council in Geneva, Switzerland. A report that raised worries with respect to the gatherings present at the meeting.

In their comments, agents of numerous nations encouraged the United States to regard fundamental basic freedoms realities. They likewise communicated their profound anger at the American act of "two-fold norms" for political closures in the space of human rights and encouraged them to confront their own privileges issues.

Simultaneously, fights racial segregation and police viciousness proceeded in numerous spots in the United States, featuring the fraud of "American-style common liberties."

As indicated by information from the site of a US non-administrative examination association, every year from 2013 to 2019; 2.5 individuals from the white local area in 1,000,000 have been casualties of police viciousness, while for a similar example, there are 6.6 individuals in the African-American people group. This is 2.6 occasions more than that of whites. Is considerably seriously aggravating that because of the imperfections in the framework, ninety nine percent of the American cops who execute the dangerous police savagery have not been indicted.

Despite COVID-19, the nearsightedness, stubborn

inadequacy, and unreliability appeared by the US government not just caused an expected 7.1 million contaminations and in excess of 200,000 passings, yet additionally demolished racial separation, this ongoing illness of American culture.

Which has dove the American individuals into a profound basic liberties fiasco.

Information from the US Center for Disease Prevention and Control shows that the pace of COVID- 19 contamination among Latin Americans is 2.8 occasions higher than among the white local area. Also, because of the hole in admittance to clinical assets and aberrations in financial conditions, the dangers of COVID-19 contamination and demise among minorities are a lot higher than among whites.

For the sake of political interest, White House government officials have pushed for racial oppression, taken an inflexible position on migration and different issues, and saw racial issues as a device of political battle, which straightforwardly prompted the ascent of xenophobia and prejudice in American culture.

With this helpless basic liberties record in the country, it is a terrible picture for those American government officials who think they are "common freedoms safeguards" and who are intentionally taking action against different nations. While at home they don't matter the standards.

There are no basic liberties "exercise provider" in this world, and no nation should rehearse "two-fold norms" on common freedoms.

Each ought to guarantee that the privileges of every individual are regarded paying little mind to race.

Prior to censuring another country that doesn't consent, you should guarantee that consistence with principles are implemented in your domain.

As we can see President Donald Trump demolished the circumstance with his bigoted discourses which, actually, didn't quiet the tempest but instead speed up.

He can say and think, it has been clear for a long time that dark votes are fundamental in official decisions in the United States.

He has his feet against the divider, since they consider him to be a despot, a conceived bigoted who, additionally, hostile to movement.

The United States today actually has a set of experiences, without the coordinated effort of blacks this triumph probably won't have occurred.

A Democratic president couldn't have had such an arrangement of chasing blacks and outsiders so without any problem. A careless choice is consistently an all-out inability to look for a subsequent term. Mr. Trump has fizzled with his approach. Fundamentally, "People of color matter" to the individuals who overlook it.

Despite the fact that Trump had affirmed that blacks don't have the foggiest idea how to function, they are just intrigued by sexual joy yet measurements show notwithstanding his explanation that blacks, outsiders are diligent employees and have contributed vigorously to the US economy.

A straightforward thought has at last forced itself, so much that nobody dares to question it any more, in any event transparently: any offer of scorn towards a specific ethnic gathering establishes an attack against every single person.

Everybody presently concurs: when they announced that Jews, Gypsies, Slavs, and so forth, were "sub-par" to the Germanic people groups, the Nazis not just insulted their casualties. By declining to concede that human pride is unbreakable, they degraded the "predominant race" itself, diminished it to the position, corrupt and unenviable, of killers, who have never involved an unmistakable spot in the social scale.

To cause her to acknowledge this defeat, she had first to be persuaded to relinquish an amazing society, to which a crazy force subbed rough publicity, crude, revolting trademarks, self-important, blustering "creative" articulations. Incomparable duplicity: this purported "race of masters" walked in sync, permitted itself to be tamed, complied with finger and eye; idiotically tolerating to be selected, she repudiated the advantage of man, shunned having an independent mind.

She gestured at her own dishonor. Prejudice, as everybody is very much aware, actually guarantees two casualties.

However, present day man has a luxuriously assorted array to affront the pride of his kindred people. It isn't fundamental for him to summon "racial" measures to permit himself to scorn certain classifications and, through them, the entire of mankind. Accepting that he is growing up himself, he may announce that such or such a gathering is sub-par compared to him, either due to his social, strict association, or for contemplations old enough and sex, and so forth the outcome doesn't change.

White and dark families keep on living in independent areas, paying little mind to their way of life.

The Sebirs are a prosperous family from Milwaukee, the capital of Wisconsin. Graduates, with more than agreeable pay, proprietors of a huge house, they by decide to move to a poor and prevalently dark area to be nearer to their families.

Their move should just be brief: it is tied in with really focusing on their wiped out little girl. However, the Sebirs stayed away forever to their home and remained in their little duplex, "since they had a feeling that they were the place where they should have been."

Their story could be just a special case in Uncle Sam's country. Be that as it may, the Sebir are the ideal illustration of an actually grounded isolation: well off dark families stay living in neighborhoods where their relatives reside. local area, despite the fact that this area is poor.

A reality that balances mainstream thought that racial ghettos are simply because of an absence of assets and not to having a place with a racial local area. What's more, this dark/white separation is expected uniquely to a certain something: white families are not in the slightest degree for settling dark families in their areas. In 2009, the National Institute of Health distributed an examination entitled,

"Blended or dark areas were delegated less alluring as a living setting than white areas, for the whites reviewed. The presence of African Americans in an area corrupts its worth."

Subsequently, regardless of whether blacks and whites have a similar way of life, they will keep on living in very much isolated areas, dark areas being, in addition, less fortunate. In the United States, almost thirty seven percent of African-American families procuring in excess of 88,000 euros each year live in helpless areas, contrasted with nine percent of white families in a similar circumstance.

These numbers are considerably more amazing in a city like Milwaukee, where isolation was especially present before equivalent rights: fifty seven percent of dark families contrasted with six percent of white families.

Wisconsin has consistently been a locale threatening to variety in areas. In 1955, Zeddie Hyler, a youthful African-American, attempted to fabricate a house in a white neighborhood in Milwaukee: its establishments were annihilated twice, inciting him to build up 24-hour reconnaissance. Police brutality is additionally important for everyday life: on August 14, conflicts broke out in the city after the passing of a dark youth shot dead by police.

African-Americans experience issues getting to credits, regardless of above and beyond pay: in 2006, the advance refusal rate for dark families was thirty one percent contrasted with thirteen percent for whites in Milwaukee.

In 2010, the city center of New Berlin, another city in Wisconsin, attempted to execute a moderate lodging strategy in white neighborhoods to make up for the absence of variety. The dangers got prompted the undertaking being deserted, provoking the central government to record a protest against the city for bigoted approaches.

There is additionally the unavoidable vibe of being an outsider in white areas, clarified by the Brookens, another family met by *The New York Times*. Their little girl couldn't tolerate being a "dark companion" any longer. The dad was captured week by week by the police for over a month and exposed to an orderly character check. Today, they have gotten back to a dominatingly dark neighborhood where they feel more incorporated.

Prejudice and ethnic separation in the United States has been a significant marvel since frontier times and the times of subjugation. Systematized prejudice allowed White Americans rights and advantages denied to Native Americans, African-Americans, Asian-Americans to Latin-Americans. Euro-Americans (particularly Anglo-Americans) are special by law in issue of schooling, migration, casting a ballot rights, citizenship, land obtaining, and criminal procedures over a period from the seventeenth century to the 1960s.

As of now, numerous non-Protestant settler bunches from Europe - especially Jews, Irish, Poles and Italians were survivors of xenophobic avoidance and different types of ethnically-based separation in American culture.

A portion of the major racially and ethnically organized organizations incorporate bondage, Indian conflicts, Indian reservations, racial isolation, Indian private schools and internment camps. Official racial segregation was to a great extent disallowed during the twentieth century and came to be viewed as socially inadmissible and/or ethically off-base.

Prejudice is as yet reflected in financial imbalances and acquires more current and roundabout types of articulation, the most prevalent being representative bigotry. Racial definition proceeds in the space of work, lodging, training, bank advances and government.

As indicated by the United States Human Rights Network, an organization of many American common and basic liberties associations, "segregation penetrates all parts of life in the United States and reaches out to all ethnic minorities."

While the presence of subjugation ostensibly shapes the base of ensuing African-American conceptualizations, the sources of African bondage have a significant financial establishment. Among the European elites who structure public legislative issues all through the age of the Atlantic exchanging framework, there is a famous philosophy considered mercantilism or the conviction that the objectives of governmental issues are incorporated around military influence and financial riches. They consider to be of pilgrim assets as a wellspring of mineral riches and crude materials and as a method for sending out items to the host country. The Native

American populace as a workforce ends up being too little after demolition by infection and savagery. The utilization of deliberate European people groups is likewise ending up being unreasonable, expensive and hindering to homegrown business and seriousness. In contrast to past populaces, Africans are "accessible in huge numbers at costs that make manor horticulture in the Americans beneficial."

In September 1909, in light of the Springfield race mobs and all the more comprehensively to hostile to Black viciousness, a gathering of reformers including W.E.B and John Dewey assembled to establish the National Association for the Advancement of Colored People.

During the primary portion of the twentieth century, a few million African-Americans left the southern United States for the north, Midwest and west of the country in a development known as the Great Migration (1916-1930). They desire to get away from the isolation and brutality they actually endure in the South, acquire the option to cast a ballot and better everyday environments. The mechanical dynamism of the North, the work prerequisites coming about because of the strengthening of military creation during the First World War gave the conditions to this transitory wave.

From 1910-1930, the dark populace of the urban areas of Chicago, New York and Philadelphia alone expanded from 226,000 to 902,000 people. The centralization of blacks in the huge urban areas of the North prompted the development of regions with a solid African-American larger part like the South Side of Chicago or Harlem in New York.

The Great Migration was joined by a significant social exchange: melodic structures explicit toward the south of the country, for example, boogie-woogie or blues, spread toward the north. The focal point of gravity for jazz music is moving from New Orleans to Chicago and New York. The Harlem neighborhood in New York is the support of a social development known as the Harlem Renaissance, whose popularity reaches out past the nation's boundaries.

Authors Zora Neale Hurston, Langston Hughes, Claude McKay, Richard Wright and craftsmen Lois Mailou Jones, William H. Johnson, Romare Bearden and Jacob Lawrence are the fundamental agents.

Blacks have been contrasted with primates and Jews to vermin. Nonetheless, thinking about the Holocaust, Theodor Adorno had recommended that a wonder like the eradication of the Jews at Auschwitz starts when you take a gander at a slaughterhouse and let it go, disclosing to yourself that they are simply creatures.

The rationale of his thinking was basic: if an individual thinks that its genuine to butcher creatures pointlessly, he won't see an ethical issue in doing likewise to any gathering of people belittled to the position of animality.

It is straightforward why this proposal of Adorno is regularly advanced by protectors of the creature cause. In any case, what is it worth? Kimberly Costello and Gordon Hodson, two analysts from Brock University (Ontario, Canada), have recently evolved test techniques to test it. In 2010, in the wake of presenting an entire arrangement of polls to socially all around incorporated understudies, they showed that the more these people see creatures as near individuals, the more they receive an inviting mentality towards minimized gatherings, like foreigners.

In another examination, the two specialists have quite recently stretched out this kind of investigation to youngsters.

They examined the association that may exist between the manner in which kids see people corresponding to creatures and their inclination to dehumanize, or animalize, people of other ethnic causes than their own. The outcomes at that point showed that the more white kids will in general view people as better than creatures, the more they express contrary biases against dark youngsters.

As has effectively been accomplished for blacks, ladies, gay people, and so on Yet, is society prepared to acknowledge the possibility that the manner in which it treats certain individuals is impacted by the manner in which it treats creatures. Blacks are overwhelmingly viewed as creatures and have been treated thusly.

In the event that we can accept the prejudice story concocting in Europe and continuously advancing with Germanic Nazis who needed to make this marvel into their own development, give an opposite significance.

The primary objective of the Nazis is to make individuals of color strange on earth and to show that the dark animal wasn't right on earth.

To cause her to acknowledge this defeat, she had first to be persuaded to relinquish an amazing society, to which a crazy force subbed rough publicity, crude, revolting trademarks, pretentious, pompous "creative" articulations. Incomparable double dealing: this supposed "race of masters" walked in sync, permitted itself to be tamed, complied with finger and eye; moronically tolerating to be enlisted, she repudiated the advantage of man, abstained from having an independent perspective. She gestured at her own humbling. Prejudice, as everybody is very much aware, actually asserts two casualties.

Whatever the contention and the objective picked, any

demeanor of scorn puts down mankind and in this way furrows the ground on which bigotry will thrive.

Disdain for any one gathering finishes in scorn for a race, and the roads of prejudice are spearheaded by mentalities which frequently owe it nothing.

In opposition to what some ridiculous equations suggest, which redirect the significance of words, there is no "bigotry" without its terms "nigger" All individuals are similarly deserving of regard.

Conjuring age or sex to keep the profit by getting it to a class continues from the equivalent reflexes which lead to prejudice yet can't be related to it.

For in him meet all feelings of dread, all hatred, all exclusion; so that "ideal bigotry" consolidates dread and aggression towards ethnic gatherings, even more so as they are effectively recognizable by their actual appearance, language, religion, economic wellbeing. To arrive, it was fundamental, by downplaying them, to "legitimize" certain non-bigoted types of scorn.

The business who looks to utilize outsiders consistently needs to know the identity of the last mentioned, his beginning, his nationality and so on.

Accepting that he is growing up himself, he may announce that such or such a gathering is second rate compared to him, either in view of his social, strict alliance, or for contemplations old enough and sex, and so forth.

The outcome doesn't transform: it is consistently mankind itself that is belittled, mocked, and embarrassed. Bigotry will be animated.

Lodging, compensation are verification of the power of bigotry, outsiders have consistently endured disdain in migration.

Discovering convenience as settlers is definitely not something simple, it requires such a lot of exertion and complicity.

Additionally, most of proprietors are not prepared to invite these last due to their skin tone.

They don't shroud their assessment to make it clear to migrants you committed an error, in these local individuals of color are not gladly received.

We just invite white individuals like us. What's more, if the last attempts to legitimize himself to disclose to him that he is naturalized, he has his naturalization visa like her, there is no distinction that he is additionally a resident, some answer with no dread or disgrace. visa doesn't mean anything.

I met an African on my way who disclosed to me an unpleasant encounter while he was living in Italy, he was searching for a house in a space the house proprietor gave him an arrangement to visit the house when he saw it was a person of color, he advised her gruffly, here individuals like you are not gladly received, sorry, I can't lease you this house.

An agony, a failure which pushed him to leave Italy as fast as could really be expected, he had the option to comprehend that his place was not with the individuals who think and talk about predominance.

One of the principle troubles in utilizing the term is the frameworks of prejudice. Its degree is very wide and we realize that the declaration of a basic reservation as to migration or multiculturalism would today be able to be blamed for "bigot".

Since the finish of the twentieth century, the employments of the word have spread, leading to maltreatments of language ("hostile to fat", "against youthful" bigotry, and so on) The term has lost its reasonable worth, frequently ending up being an affront equipped for excluding the rival.

It ought to likewise be noticed that there is a discussion around ethnocentrism, which can't be stringently mistaken for bigotry. The mentality that this idea covers, and which can be viewed as general, will in general make the domain or the way of life of having a place the focal point of the world.

It can truth be told lead to over-esteeming them and can likewise thusly take care of disdain and narrow mindedness towards others, prompting bigotry. Intercultural instruction has frequently been considered as a remedy to ethnocentrism, anyway it involves the danger of legitimizing a social relativism watching out for differentialism. The definition and treatment of contrast are thusly at the core of the intricacy of the marvel of "prejudice."

Bigotry shows up under four perspectives: it shows itself in mentalities (remarks, affronts, dangers, and so on) in light of assessments, convictions, enunciated in generalizations and biases; it is likewise found in practices that are communicated through friendly works on going from evasion to mistreatment, in coordinated or sloppy structures; it additionally exists through methods of activity that regulate rejection, isolation, segregation (state oppression, politically-sanctioned racial segregation, and so forth); at long last, it shows itself as philosophical, hypothetical, even dogmatic talks, comprised of accounts pointed toward legitimizing the mastery of certain human gatherings by others, and frequently alluding to science for this reason.

In France, the Pleven law of July 1, 1972 lawfully characterizes bigotry as "affectation to separation, contempt or brutality against an individual or a gathering of individuals due to their beginning or of their having a place, or not having a place with a particular ethnic gathering, country, race or religion."

Bigotry starts with an organic premise. Surmising the presence of human gatherings called "races", he hypothesizes that the individuals from each "race" share practically speaking a hereditary legacy which decides their scholarly aptitudes and their ethical characteristics. Researchers and literati clarify that these "races" would be progressive as indicated by the nature of this legacy, which would give on some of them the right, if not the obligation, to rule the others.

The Second World War, in its eradicating measurement, generally added to excluding the natural establishments of prejudice. Under the heaviness of good, political, logical and legitimate judgments, bigotry has gone through changes.

It has developed: bigoted mentalities, practices and addresses currently target societies, some being deprecated and others esteemed. We at that point discuss "social bigotry", which is communicated today more in an emblematic and hidden manner.

There is additionally a neo-prejudice, "differentialist", which doesn't biologize or hierarchize human gatherings, yet commends characters and backers the distance, or even the shortfall of contact, between these gatherings.

Numerous countries have advanced without in a general sense refreshing the product of their aggregate creative mind influenced by a bigotry acquired from pioneer and slave culture.

Many are the people still detainees of an obsolete aggregate creative mind which, now and again, liberates the profundities of their scorn for the "Savages" and the overwhelmed of yesterday.

Joyce Echaquan's inauspicious takeoff severely carries the issue of bigotry to the surface. For ages, regardless of a horde of laws and political activities, we have still not prevailing with regards to annihilating this disaster. We all are more frequently bolted on the outcomes of this scourge instead of on its sources.

Prejudice isn't a behavioral condition. It is the declaration of the social engraving acquired from colonization and bondage. An engraving that decided the request for the world and established the standards of our countries.

Western perspectives in the eighteenth and nineteenth hundreds of years had disguised a world request dependent on bigoted biases that have made due through time.

As per investigators, to censure our contemporary bigots, it would initially be important to bring out and question the chain of disguised social components which adapted them and which underlie their wrongdoings.

We need to address History. Specifically the job of the supposed "pioneers" of the Americas who brought "native examples" back to Europe. They gave material to slander and abuse the researchers and amazing European "ethnocentrics" of the time.

The pseudo study of the eighteenth and nineteenth hundreds of years is at the base of bigotry. She dissected, estimated and ordered the Other; the extraordinary. The "callous savage". She developed the supposed races. She arranged, indexed, and classified human gatherings.

She established the bigoted talk that has filled strict, political and aggregate imaginaries over the ages.

Pioneer publicity set up that there are dominants and ruled. This hefty social legacy has been passed down from one age to another until now.

The universe of culture, expressions of the human experience and letters of the time was not to be outshone. Allow us to think specifically of the Hollywood symbolism that has organized and molded the aggregate creative mind in America and all throughout the planet. The great cattle rustlers and the "awful Indians". The evil African "man-eaters"...

The creation of an "ethnocentric" aggregate creative mind has excluded the other more than a few ages.

Against bigotry and disdain discourse laws restrict and preclude segregation and disdain discourse. They give a decent heart. Nonetheless, they don't change hearts.

It would initially be important to deconstruct bigoted talk and generalizations. To address what has truly, socially, experimentally, strictly, and politically adapted the look on the Other. It goes through family, school, culture and the media.

Strategically, the main dark individuals from the United States Congress were chosen under the Republican mark in November 1868, three years after the annulment of subjugation. It was not until 1934 that the Democratic Party introduced its first dark competitors.

From 1936-1966, in any event 2,800 blacks were killed in lynchings. The province of North Carolina set up a constrained disinfection program focusing on blacks somewhere in the range of 1929 and 1974. 7,600 individuals, including youngsters, were casualties.

During the Great Depression of the 1930s, African Americans were especially hard hit by joblessness and neediness. In the event that the New Deal dispatched by President Franklin Delano Roosevelt made no particular arrangement for them, dark Americans exploited different projects and government help: for instance, they got thirty three percent of lodging help. It was from this time that they changed their political association, going more to Roosevelt's gathering, the Democratic coalition.

The circumstance of African-Americans is gradually improving: their social mix is advancing because of the military during World War II (700,000 blacks in the military in 1944). Maybe, the contention against the Axis powers would in general weld the country together, despite the fact that race riots broke out in 1943. Roosevelt found a way to restrict them in the government organization (Executive Order 880). In 1942, the Congress of Racial Equality is established to battle against separation in open structures in the North of the country. The Great Migration that started in the Interwar Period proceeds: a few thousand blacks leave the South to work in the Californian cities. In 1941, pioneers of the association, including Asa Philip Randolph, induced the government to begin integrating the processing plants in the north by compromising and organizing mass protest marches in the capital.

The initial steps against isolation were taken in the southern states after World War II, given the African-American-upheld war exertion in the nation's military. In 1949, the military entered a period of all out integration. On account of the endeavors of African-American legal advisor Thurgood Marshall and the NAACP, school isolation was proclaimed illegal by the United States Supreme Court in 1954 (Brown v. Leading body of Education). The other Jim Crow laws were canceled by the Civil Rights Act of 1964 and the Voting Rights Act. Highly contrasting relationships were authorized across the United States in 1967 by a Supreme Court administering.

The 1960s are set apart by the figure of Martin Luther King (1929-1968) who coordinated and drove walks for the option to cast a ballot, minority work, and other essential social liberties for African Americans. He is most popular for his "I have a fantasy" discourse on August 28, 1963 before the Lincoln Memorial in Washington during the March for Jobs and Freedom. He meets John F. Kennedy who upholds him in the battle against racial separation.

Martin Luther King and the social liberties development, in any case, are not valued by general assessment and the walk is dismissed by sixty six percent of Americans. As per surveys completed in 1964, New Yorkers consider Martin To be King as an "radical" and consider the requests for social equality "unreasonable". In 1963, fifty nine percent of white individuals said they were agreeable to restricting interracial relationships, fifty-five percent wouldn't live close to individuals of color, and ninety percent went against their little girl dating one of them. In 1966, the citizens of California got by submission the abrogation of arrangements good for the racial blend of lodging. The integration takes a savage turn with various deaths, riots in specific urban communities and in the ghettos: somewhere in the range of 1965 and 1968, the brutality left two fifty dead and eight thousand injured all through the country. In 1968, a report by the Kerner Commission took a gander at the reasons for this brutality and addressed the beginning stage of the arrangement of positive segregation.

The first to utilize the expression Affirmative Action is US President John Fitz Gerald Kennedy; it was then taken over by his replacement in the White House, Lyndon B. Johnson. Their thought was that, regardless of balance laws, individuals of color would in any case linger behind the remainder of the American populace.

The point was to guarantee that blacks were more

addressed in talented positions, colleges, the media, and so on. From the 1960s, particular positions were set up. In any case, it is in no way, shape or form a strategy of portions: In 2003, the Supreme Court censured the rule of standards as being in opposition to fairness under the watchful eye of the law and to free rivalry. The outcomes are viewed as persuading in the United States: in 1960, thirteen percent of African- Americans had a place with the working classes, they are sixty six percent in 2000.

The quantity of blacks in the working class has quadrupled and the quantity of helpless blacks has divided. Ethnic incongruities are additionally a lot more grounded in Latin-America, which in any case has gained notoriety for crossbreeding.

Today we are seeing an uneven and sensational legislative issues: prejudice and scorn for the other are increasingly acknowledged. What was absolutely inconceivable, unsatisfactory today is viewed as resilience and ordinary. Mankind and common liberties, opportunity of love and law and order are transparently enduring an onslaught. It is an assault, which concerns us all. We know the meaning of the Landtag races in Saxony and Saxon relations for the encounter in the push of the privilege at the government level. All of Europe is caught by a patriot talk that advances doubt and prohibition.

The marvel of migration is evidence of this mind boggling reality. We without a doubt can't help thinking about why such countless outsiders look for asylum in Europe, in the United States, in Canada.

The explanation is basic, its frantic outsiders are dismissed in their nation of cause by the specialists who have abused their privilege and still keep on accepting, there is just one expectation, "the excursion."

They have the data that everything is working out in a good way in these nations, the occupants and the outsiders are filled in that to be a superior life, they are prepared to give their life to find this fortune. The specialists should have a reasonable strategy for an open and joined society where common liberties are legitimate for all and where variety and self-assurance of life projects are clear. We should go against all types of cruel treatment, separation and viciousness.

Individuals who know about the fortitude of society ought not be utilized against one another.

Regardless of whether at the lines of Europe, in a state of banishment associations or welcome activities, whether in strange, women's activist or hostile to bigoted developments, in associations on the side of outcasts, whether in worker's organizations, affiliations, NGOs, strict or neighborhood networks, whether it is the obligation to one side to lodging, the option to admittance to medical care, against checking and the hardening of laws, against the hardship of exile rights and for environment value. We should secure displaced people, foreigners on the off chance that they look for unique consideration that they couldn't discover in their local land.

Allow us to hold hands with the people in question and backing them!

The pandemic should fill in as an exercise and join us. Since the beginning of the lockdown, a genuine scorn for class has been shown all over the place. In the media, on informal organizations and in the articulations of legislators, the authorities appear to be the ideal decision: The occupants of common areas disdained embarrassed deserted.

Tight controls in the neighborhoods where ethnic minorities are more gigantic over ten percent of the verbalizations and the admonitions worry for the first day of constrainment in quite a while.

The control zones are "focused" as indicated by the police, numerous reports of bigoted checks and police assaults against racialized individuals during the checks have effectively been accounted for. The legitimacy or in any case of the justification go left to the carefulness of the police will in general advance disparities in the treatment of non-repression between advantaged or average areas.

The individuals who are viewed as poor, the voiceless are the people in question.

On the off chance that the media appear to show a specific altruism towards individuals having a place with the working class and the Bourgeoisie, it isn't about individuals living in dubiousness. As usual, and surprisingly more obvious in the time frame, it is ethnic minorities and living in average neighborhoods who are hit hardest by the suppression. In the event that checks, fines and police savagery were at that point the standard before the beginning of the pandemic, presently the COVID gives further avocation to these works on, pushing the bad habit to the purpose of putting individuals in police guardianship on the simple doubt and further expanding the wellbeing hazards for caught individuals. They are the primary casualties of standards, of norms.

The reality of restriction, a class advantage for VIPs not for needy individuals as indicated by certain eyewitnesses.

On the off chance that constrainment appears to be a lovely route for everybody to be capable without a lot of trouble for the good, having had the option to leave their condos for second homes (conceivably conveying the infection to places where it was not at this point), it is an entire distinctive matter for those and the individuals who previously lived in instability. To be sure, how not to be moved by daily routine secured for families experiencing together in unsanitary and/or little convenience, without gallery or nursery, when others disclose to us the "karma" that such a circumstance can address period to check out their life.

Along these lines, it isn't unexpected to go over individuals in the roads. The state, with its opposing directives, just builds up this situation. In the common areas, among the populaces coming about because of migration and colonization, numerous and many are problematic specialists, the lowest pay permitted by law workers, who proceed to work and place their wellbeing and that of their families at serious risk, forfeited on the special stepped area of private enterprise (without failing to remember the individuals who have been made jobless and who will lose a piece of their pay further debasing everyday environments).

Contempt Repeated Arguments

The substitutes change, however the rationale stays as before. On the off chance that we had the option to notice a blast of hostile to Asian bigotry in the beginning of the emergency, today it is every one of those viewed as outside the public and conservative agreement who are influenced by these rationales. The state is executing its administration of the pestilence in "conservative reconquest" neighborhoods in a postcolonial rationale. Undoubtedly, the news returns us to scenes in pilgrim history when "native" populaces were considered "unrestrained" and for whom constrainment was more extreme. Likewise, the media and political figures develop and disperse a talk that intends to make blameworthy and to assign as dependable a piece of the populace, racialized and having a place with the famous classes, depicted as "wayward" and "oblivious."

For them, it is tied in with restricting racialized populaces – associated with spreading the infection – to "genuine French individuals" prone to be contaminated, debilitated or in grieving. This manner of speaking is even more degraded as it looks to dehumanize some portion of the populace by preventing the truth from getting their encounters during this emergency, and by the way the truth of the much really glaring well-being challenges of medical clinics in some helpless urban areas.

This bigoted brutality serves to veil the failings of force, both regarding the disappointment of past metropolitan and against social arrangements, and its cataclysmic administration of the wellbeing emergency. It is additionally in a setting of long-standing pressures and a specific doubt of the populaces towards a force and a police power which detest them, prohibit them and abuse them for quite a long time, that the police viciousness is exacerbated.

No circumstance, even outstanding, will legitimize the suppression and the assignment of a classification of the populace, in light of its group or its roots, as mindful. Despite this current, we should not be tricked by foes, just self-association and fortitude between tricky individuals will permit us to receive in return, regardless of whether even with restraint or disconnection.

As an update: to battle police brutality, recordings permit individuals to affirm. The "Police Violence Emergency" application makes it conceivable specifically to record these recordings on a worker to protect proof.

A scene happens in a nursery in Waregem. Two youngsters, matured ten and thirteen, find their neighbor peeing through the fence isolating the two properties.

"My younger sibling got down on him," says Ismail, the most established kin who didn't go to the scene. She advised him: "It isn't done, it isn't typical. In the event that you need to pee, go to your latrine. "The neighbor at that point began to affront my sibling and my sister," tossing "Grimy niggers, you smell." My sister answered that in any event we were peeing in our latrines, and not in our neighbors' nurseries.

While the youthful teen isn't let somewhere near the neighbor, the other kid films the trade with his cell phone. We can unmistakably hear the bigoted affronts: "Messy niggers, you smell! Return to your country! four out of five Belgians at this point don't need you here."

Ismail isn't astonished by his neighbor's conduct, despite the fact that he laments that he is assaulting kids. "He could never say that to me, for instance, since I don't figure he would dare say that to grown-ups. We attempted to converse with him, yet he won't ever open. In any event, when you are certain it is, he is at home, he doesn't set out to open the entryway.

This isn't the first occasion when that Ismail's family, of Moroccan cause, has been focused by the neighbor. "At the point when we travel in the late spring, he tosses a ton of trash in our nursery. For instance, trash from his trees that he prunes. Indeed, even now, when he smokes a cigarette, he tosses it in our home. He generally attempts to incite us, to stand out."

This time, Ismail chose not to stop there. "My folks and I don't care for contending with neighbors. You generally need to attempt to manage everything well. Yet, this was pointless excess, we needed to accomplish something."

The police ordered it as a "basic contention" and not prejudice.

The youngster professes to have stopped an objection with the police. "They arranged the protest as 'simply a contention' and not prejudice." So Ismail kept in touch with Unia, the Equal Opportunities Center. The head of the Center, Patrick Charlier, clarifies that oral affronts have been decriminalized in Belgium since the 2000s, and along these lines rely upon every district. "It was an issue of putting need on the city managerial assents. We should check whether, in Waregem, such endorses can be taken."

The battle against bigotry has developed and changed impressively in ongoing many years. Impacted by the ascent of global assembly around the idea of common freedoms, its directions and accomplishments are basically founded on the public political culture in which it is inserted. The discussions of the last worldwide meeting against bigotry, held in 2001 in Durban, vouch for the challenges in tracking down a typical language on the issue notwithstanding the heterogeneity of definitions relying upon the country and the gatherings of people concerned.

Take the instance of Brazil and France. The legend of racial popular government in Brazil is by all accounts something contrary to the French fantasy of the Republic. The primary makes the concordance of relations between the races, which is supposed to be the product of the numerous interbreeding that has denoted the historical backdrop of Brazil, a mainstay of popular government.

This story, which has steadily been built since the abrogation of subjugation, pretty much rules out acknowledgment of bigotry, the actual presence of which is continually addressed. The portion of prejudice and the manner in which it shows itself in the public eye are still inadequately characterized in a country where almost forty five percent of the populace is dark.

The French conservative fantasy, pervaded with the soul of the Enlightenment, advocates the putting to the side of all social particularism to guarantee the equivalent treatment of residents. Conservative standards ensure a requesting cautiousness and judgment of bigotry while restricting the discussion on the very classifications that the marvel brings into play. The difficulty of considering contrasts dependent on source, nationality, or religion in insights restricts the creation of an outline and conditions the acknowledgment of racial segregation.

This background, explicit to every nation, gives us a first thought of the troubles in estimating bigotry and fighting it. It permits, in addition to other things, to all the more likely comprehend the idea of the hole saw in Brazil as in France between the advancement of enactment, different legal assets to battle against bigotry and segregation and their application.

These instruments can to be sure remain generally disregarded by the organizations just as by the people expected to utilize them.

On the two sides of the Atlantic, methods of understanding bigotry have carried such a determinism to the people in question, in different ways getting them far from the issue. The lived insight of the casualties has since a long time ago stayed in the shadow of the misfortunes and injuries of the past or of the social inquiry. Direct help to casualties infers truth be told the acknowledgment of a humiliating topicality of racial segregation which raises doubt about the profound working of society and its establishments and dangers undermining the establishments of its popularity based practice.

After some time, the extraordinary changes occurring inside these two social orders have molded another attitude toward prejudice and racial separation by pushing public activity to zero in increasingly more on the people who endure them. Specifically, the imperativeness of ethnic, social and strict character confirmations, discernible in Brazil as in France, gives new profundity to the subject of bigotry.

From reprobation to assuming responsibility for one's lived insight, the fundamental phases of hostile to bigoted activity in the two nations uncover the cycles of development and deconstruction of the no encompassing the acknowledgment of prejudice, to a great extent affected by their public political culture. Today, the old standardizing structures are not, at this point adequate to contain the battle against bigotry, which is conveyed in a space crossed by various lines of strain platform from the worldwide to the staff, and challenge the activity of the 'State' around here.

Racial order, in view of shading, just becomes an integral factor afterward, as it is controlled by the social circumstance of people. "White" and "dark" relate to financial positions, to such an extent that upward versatility reclassifies a person's skin tone.

This is the reason, as Pierson notes, "Branco" (white) alludes to an individual who is white yet paying little mind to their racial foundation, including every one of the individuals who, blended race or dark, have a place with the privileged societies. The assignment "preto" alludes both to actual qualities and to having low economic wellbeing. Nonetheless, social versatility is low and most of blacks stay at the lower part of the social stepping stool.

After some time, the social perusing of race relations develops further for both political and philosophical reasons. In the second fifty percent of the 1940s, Gilberto Freyre combined the legend of racial majority rule government by acting interbreeding like the assurance of the solidarity of the Brazilian public. In a worldwide political setting actually shaken by despotism, he takes advantage of the chance to shape an uncommon majority rule articulation that separates itself from Western qualities and conflicts with the perspectives guarded by the negritude development. Simultaneously, sociology examines, generally impacted by the class battle worldview, underline the social character of imbalances.

In France, the vote based fantasy that impacts originations

of bigotry appears to be exceptionally far taken out from the Brazilian setting. The post-war period dives the country into a verifiable change tapped by the worldview of the Jewish decimation. On the off chance that in Brazil the discussion is basically at the scholarly level, it is growing more in France on the political and social ground.

The battle against prejudice comprises most importantly in remembering the idea of basic liberties for sacred writings. Saturated with the conservative soul, the judgment of bigotry includes putting to the side social, ethnic and strict particularities in the public space. Congruity inside society is in this manner dependent on a guideline of equity adapted by the ideal of eradicating contrasts. In accordance with the Declaration of the Rights of Man and of the Citizen of 1789, the Constitution of October 4, 1958 specifies in its first article that "France is a unified, common, vote based and social Republic. It guarantees fairness under the steady gaze of the law for all residents without differentiation of root, race or religion. She regards all convictions."

The infection of wokeness and character legislative issues at last tainted individuals' psyches, and colleges barely empowered discussion any longer, they secure the musings of bigots, enemies of bigots longed for a reality where race had only of equivalent significance.

Everybody is conceived equivalent in law, says a Black says a White. Today, enemies of bigots can't sit around and let it go again and again.

To stop the topic of race which overwhelms and is the subject of regular daily existence, the bigots should acknowledge the absolute situation unequivocally.

Each one of the individuals who profess not to feel the

plague, heard the commotion, the calls of the casualties who can presently don't take it, "it's false reverence" Just also the accessories claim not to know.

For them, the variety clarifies everything. It is the alpha and omega of our personality. It decides all that we are.

In contrast to Martin Luther King, they don't pass judgment on individuals by their character, their activities or their thoughts, yet by the shade of their skin.

For some bigoted whites, blacks just have terrible considerations. For some bigoted blacks, they think they are better than whites.

Interesting, this is by and large some's opinion: that there is a dark "substance" that recognizes blacks from whites.

We can't talk about bigoted gatherings from such a time. The bigots will not change the tone and furthermore, to alter their perspectives. They would prefer not to nullify the idea of race. They need to amplify it, commend it, sublimate it, and misuse it even today.

Make it fundamental. Grow it until it occupies all the room.

George Floyd was murdered on the grounds that he was dark. At the point when his professional killer took a gander at him, this is the thing that he saw. Not an individual, but rather a dark.

This is the explanation we were so vexed. The passing of George Floyd is substantial evidence of this scourge which is the bigot. They carry on the beat of the white race, the strong, the lone genuine race.

A conversation on bigotry, as also on sexism or ageism (hostile to old or against youthful), and on subjection, can possibly occur when the social entertainers understand its... presence.

Contrasting one race with another the reverse way around is regular bigotry. We can't invest our energy looking at an understudy from France, Canada with those from a country in the Caribbean, from Africa who are in a school, college that has the exemplary supplies and materials to follow exercises. The outcome won't ever go back.

This is obviously a strength, which experiences incredible exemptions, in one course as in the other (the situation with ladies as slaves, besides, change starting with one space or time then onto the next ...) There have been thinkers since Antiquity to question the benefits of treating men distinctively as indicated by the shade of their skin, similarly as there are still philosophies today which "build up" fundamental contrasts between "races". On the off chance that in friendly relations, blacks are mistreated by whites, the degree of conflictuality ascends as the state of one another represents an issue, and particularly as their differential societal position starts to fluctuate quickly, for some reasons which can be just financial or strict.

This doesn't mean, and this is additionally one of the standards of conflictology that we might want to feature, that these contentions didn't exist previously, however they can be communicated in an inexorably open way, as much by the attention to the individuals who are essential for the prevailing classes of the treachery of the situation exclusively by the refusal of the individuals who are important for the overwhelmed classes to keep on enduring similar shameful acts and a similar viciousness. There must be sure conditions for the situation to be challenged, for what stayed stowed away from the eyes of everything is uncovered, to turn into a wellspring of social battles or all the more precisely to utilize a stylish articulation, of battles. cultural. These go past the monetary system and also confuse every one of the clashing fields of society, the various sorts of conflictuality having a tendency to blend.

It is from the impression of who is "bigot" and of what is "savage" that another field of open struggles between gatherings of people is conceived. It is with this thought that Paul ZAWADZKI's appearance on bigotry starts. "Where does this viciousness start, what are its shapes? Conveyed by a detonated lexical field, the word bigotry experiences semantic over-burden."

Gordon W ALLPORT (The idea of Prejudice, 1954) recognizes a few kinds of bigoted conduct, in a general public where exactly the "racial inquiry" is in the frontal area. Verbal dismissal, aversion, segregation, actual assaults (racial mobs, lynchings, massacres...) killing. "Whatever the sort of society, the brutality of the annihilation of individuals and property is certain for those on whom it is applied.

Then again, as to the initial three sorts, the viciousness is for the most part stopped in the hole between the law and the reality. Hence, rehearses which violate the guideline of equivalent rights show up "normally" to be viciously oppressive in libertarian social orders, at any rate to the individuals who share its establishments. Alternately, a fixed detachment of spots, spaces and praises, lead of partition or evasion, confidence in prevalence dependent on the nature or the past of a given gathering, appear to identify with the idea of things in social orders represented by the progressive standard where "the overall thought of comparative is dark" (Tocqueville).

On the size of the hundreds of years, the concurrence by

various leveled interlocking is shockingly steady, and nothing forestalls to imagine that various gatherings lived agreeably under a different legitimate system as long as this standard appeared to be normal to them (approved, adequate, self-evident...) "Bigotry as an issue emerges in social orders which, slowly dismissing the possibility of an fundamental common distinction, consider people rises to, comparative.

Equity standards are adequately fundamental to deliver ill-conceived biased practices dependent on obvious actual contrasts. This investigation is reasonably broadly shared (LEGROS, 1999; MESURE, RENAUT, 1999). As indicated by Pierre-André TAGUIEFF, it is in the portrayals of Eluesinian social orders and of Nazi Germany that the utilization of "prejudice" created. Yet, well before, regarding the matter of bondage, discussions of a similar sort before as of now emerged. The disclosure of the Americas by European guides without a doubt incited the initially systematized discusses: are the "Indians" men (offspring of God)? Regardless, it would be the development, the change to innovation that makes the conditions for the chance of bigoted spasms. For Anna AREND (The Origins of Totalitarianism), "it is correctly the new idea of balance that makes current relations between races so troublesome." more grounded presence of bigoted bias in the States which have formally nullified servitude, Louis DUMONT details "the easiest theory which is to assume that bigotry reacts, in another structure, with an old capacity. Everything occurs as though it addressed, in populist society, a resurgence of what was communicated in an unexpected way, more straightforwardly and normally, in progressive society. Make the qualification ill-conceived and you have separation, eliminate old methods of differentiation, and you have bigoted belief system." Anti-populist hatred, as Norbert ELIAS puts it, is connected to the "racial" question.

Be that as it may, the subject of making a move brings up issues. In the event that bigotry can be communicated as bias, philosophy, pseudo-logical defense, or be encapsulated in works on going from isolation to kill, there would be no relationship of need among bias and practice of segregation (experience of Richard T LaPiere of 1934 revealed in Social powers, n ° 13). Beside the way that the reasons given by singular killers are incredibly factor, it is hard to regard them as simple defenses. For each situation, diverse examination ideal models are activated. An assemblage of exploration prepares psychoanalytic ideas and approaches issues of dissatisfactions and substitutes. The investigation of cases in which aggregate viciousness is exposed reveals insight into the way that they occur in emergency circumstances, where the State is regularly falling flat or even that it diverts famous revolts along these lines.

Regardless, bigotry is a diverse marvel, including components that are not really associated. What do a horde of insane whites who lynch an individual of color following a criminal demonstration in a modest community in the South of the United States share practically speaking with the cool precise killing, in view of "logical" ideas, of whole populaces? We can manage bigoted mentalities or practices legitimized "experimentally" similarly as with practices guided exclusively by mental disdain in close to home or aggregate circumstances whose causes are "recognized" in socially various individuals assigned distinctly through the shade of their skin. It appears to be that the expression "bigotry" is utilized for altogether different practices that solitary the utilization of skin tone normalizes. Regardless, it isn't by adding bigotry to against Semitism that the discussion will be cleared up.

Patrick Tort proposes a meaning of prejudice which shows how wide the scope of practices is: "Can be qualified as bigoted any talk which addresses the eventual fate of human gatherings as dominatingly administered by local organic disparities - fixed or developing - , following up on it in the way of a natural, persevering, contagious and actuating determinism, approving or endorsing practices planned to achieve or support the results of the underlying chains of importance that this talk hypothesizes. " The hypothesize of natural imbalance is along these lines comprised of exact properties. Charles Darwin trained professional, whose enemy of bigoted idea he likewise underlines, cautions against the shortcoming of contemporary enemy of bigotry. It isn't sufficient to deny the contrasts between human gatherings - he ventures to such an extreme as to caution against the invalidation of races - an assessment that we don't share, in a contention which isn't inadequate in exactness.

"Other than that, no genuine naturalist," he composed, couldn't keep up that races don't exist, the investigation of genotypes and hemotypology can't, in law, cause us to fail to remember the degree of living beings, and naturalistic human studies, similarly. good judgment properly denies. The forswearing of reality in regards to the presence of race and races is in logical inconsistency with the trifling, however not unimportant, truth that these are aggregates that occupy human social orders, and that these aggregates are different. For their part, the studies of man and society catch connections among socially and socially coordinated human people, and not connections of more prominent or lesser nearness between bunches Certainly, the improvement of trades and the versatility of people has supported a solid interbreeding, the advancement of which profoundly relativizes the legitimacy of any assertion concerning the "virtue" of races, as of now relativized in itself by r the straightforward certainty of development. Yet, the reality stays that apparent racial contrasts remain which comprise the magnificence and the hold of polymorphism of mankind, and which one can adore as such as opposed to deciding to demolish them. The most fitting response to deliver to pseudo-reformist enemy of bigotry which will in general implicate prejudice as drivel beginning from the supposed natural non-presence of race, hence appears as an inquiry: and assuming race existed, would-is it genuine to be a bigot?

Our booking comes from the way that bigoted talk overall is a lot less fortunate than this reflection on the genotype or the aggregate, some of the time verging on being a basic defense of criminal realities. It is the basic juxtaposition of the view of the refusal to be socially mediocre particularly showed by gatherings or people of various tone since this is the fundamental basis recently submitted and of the semi mandatory closeness which incites in specific gatherings and certain individuals. people "bigot reflexes", considerably more frequently as remarks "jokes" than acts.

Moreover, the phenotypic contrast can't be absorbed to a genotypic distinction, which would prompt examining human races and not the human species. A fundamental basis, and this is the thing that makes bigoted responses so irate, is that these supposed races blend effectively when they ought to as indicated by them organically be incongruent... That is, in bigotry, even logical, the combination of the social and the regular, which makes any univocal methodology troublesome. All the time, besides, bigotry is generally controlled in populaces that are socially ineffectively instructed and educated regarding the real factors of the world by others considerably more edified on the conspicuous troubles of utilizing a logically based bigoted language... what's more, who don't stop for a second, in a covered manner, to "taste" frequently fleshly wealth present in "different races."

The blended couple isn't in every case liberated from bigotry. Try not to be tricked by the figment that these associations are insusceptible to segregation.

The new debates and the accomplishment on dating applications vouch for the fetishization of which racialized individuals can be the item. On the web or, all things considered, they are at times treated as encounters to be tried and regularly need to manage unbridled generalizations and exoticization. Indeed, even at the upper phase of a relationship, they are not generally resistant.

Concerned individuals recount the fixation of a portion of their accomplices or who were for separating prosaisms and recollect the dehumanizing examinations they have heard considerably under the covers. Among exoticization and downgrading, prejudice meddles in the closeness of certain blended couples.

At the end of the day, it implies accepting that segregation is the worry of a couple of people and that it isn't important for a bigger reality; it is to believe that bigotry isn't foundational and that adoration, similar to a safeguard, would have the option to end the outer impact applied by an inconsistent society. Foundations, culture, porn and publicizing barrage us with racial generalizations that can have repercussions in the private circle - heartfelt connections are not generally saved.

At some point, a man goes over a befuddling instant message sent by his ex to a companion. She clarified how, during their sex, she came to appreciate because of her "creature power" and depicted impressions of "uncommon hostility."

From the outset complimented, he rapidly understands that this kind of alternate way is comparably continuous as it is hazardous. "She was exceptionally shocked that I could make reference to a name, Mr. H or Mr. K during our conversations." When he attempts to make her mindful of it, the banalities downpour much more: "She answered that I was unique since I communicated well and that I should take it for a commendation, since it is an uncommon quality at "we."

On the off chance that these couples have for some time been untouchable, even restricted, their expansion shows that the lines are moving. For certain individuals, their minimization would even be an instant answer for counter prejudice.

As Robin Zheng calls attention to, most conversations of prejudice in the private circle "rotate around if it is brought about by pessimistic racial generalizations." As if sincere goals have the ability to abrogate any prejudicial measurement and the results it suggests on the people concerned. The photos ought to be taken as praises. Fetishization would just be a somewhat complimenting matter of inclination.

Albeit explicit dreams should be recognized from relational connections, "it happens that a portion of these connections are persuaded by buzzwords or by the craving to overcome racialized bodies which are outlandish." To legitimize themselves, individuals don't stop for a second to diminish this fetishization to a basic matter of taste, just as an inclination for fair hair or green eyes. This is the manner by which we end up with a Yann Moix who gloats of just dating Asians and an individual disclosing to be experiencing "wilderness fever" to legitimize his selective appreciation for dark and blended race ladies.

The bad faith around the inquiry, don't accept a lot of the individuals who profess to need to help battle this scourge, frequently they need to communicate to show the business of this marvel.

Yet, I guarantee you, they are numerous content with this lifestyle, an arrangement by class of individual to the detriment of their race.

They are enchanted to have everything, to be satisfied, they think they are above, better than a gathering of people.

Their perspective is clear, they have basically no boundaries, they needn't bother with any visa to visit most of the alleged immature nations. The specialists of their nation ensure that they are all around directed VIPs.

They depend on every one of the standards to legitimize the predominance of race. But then, the specialists ought to rapidly change the circumstance since there are many hitched residents with the passport, they are naturally recipients paying little mind to their skin tone, identity, race and so forth.

One lady clarified her story, the bigotry of the last's ex-accomplice combined with practically non-existent sexism is reflected in the practically deliberate relationship of certain character characteristics with their inceptions. At the point when I pulled away, he claimed not to remember me and the contention broke out, "reviews the 28-year-old." Since it isn't generally conceivable to perceive or comprehend this relationship, prejudice experienced outside of the relationship can be a test. Now and again, one may even disparage or belittle the possibility of color visual impairment, accepting that social race is superfluous, which empowers the forswearing of the subsequent racial bias. Recognize their advantages.

Would they be able to shape associations with men washed in a social climate that makes misogynist pride? Sometimes, this can turn into a test, if certainly feasible. White individuals regularly love a person of color wholeheartedly, but since individuals around him don't acknowledge this relationship, he is compelled to surrender.

"It relies upon the accomplices to bring issues to light to stop the couple's bigotry." She said: "In spite of her conduct, my companions actually don't comprehend why I need to remain with my ex." truly, I don't generally acknowledge it and I am profoundly infatuated.

"By tuning in to biased discourses about their physical and character characteristics, ethnic minorities some of the time come to disguise these predispositions to the degree that they are set as standards." notwithstanding brutality, we don't really need to discover and discover an answer. "Feeling doesn't make thinking simple. At the point when you're passionate it can in some cases become harder to recognize these issues." It takes mindfulness, at that point an impact. "Solving the issue of racial separation among ethnic minorities isn't focused on minorities, however the accomplices should tackle the issue all alone."

It's an account of disdain and lip service for the couple, since, in such a case that you know your heart well you will not cherish somebody since you feel predominant, why you need an encounter that doesn't great. Since where it counts in your heart you don't care for that individual and don't coexist with them, so there is some sort of interest, either in their actual excellence or in the sexual maltreatment they are exposed to. Essentially, just this swashbuckler can clarify something noticeable or undetectable. He doesn't care for his sweetheart's dark skin, yet he prefers her delicate skin.

We should dissect the meaning of the term 'sexual maltreatment to comprehend the earnestness of the racial issue.

Kid sexual maltreatment is any demonstration of a sexual sort that damages or dangers hurting a kid or young lady, genuinely or inwardly, including a grown-up accomplice or another youngster. It regularly includes substantially contact, however not generally (presentation, moral requirement or youngster porn). These activities establish offenses or wrongdoings which are immovably rebuffed in many nations.

Hence, as indicated by the bond (family, instructive) between them, the conditions, the country, and the sexual relations with a minor under the lawful age can establish an offense or a wrongdoing. A few nations denounce the relationship even with another minor, however for the most part endure it if the age contrast is little.

In Europe, the time of fluctuates somewhere in the range of 14 and 18 years. Mandate 2011/93/EU of the European Parliament and of the Council on fighting the sexual maltreatment and sexual misuse of kids, just as youngster erotic entertainment characterizes defensive measures and least punishments to be set in every Member State.

In France, the time of sexual greater part is 15 years of age, however the grown-up submits an offense in the event that he has a relationship with a consenting individual younger than eighteen, on the off chance that he is an ascendant or has expert on the minor by excellence of his capacity or if the minor is a weak individual.

Then again, this relationship, unreservedly agreed by the minor, should not be defaced by explicit conditions which make it culpable: compensation in cash or in kind (prostitution), instigation to intemperance or erotic entertainment, avoidance of parental position.

There are secret affiliations that work with adolescent young ladies regularly are those from Africa, promising to crown them, to cause them to turn into a model and so on.

These young ladies and ladies who showed up in Europe as a model will rapidly be changed over into whores.

Because of an absence of training, they didn't request data about their visit, and their fantasy is to get comfortable one of the Schengen territories to make this blessing from heaven.

These mafias focused on explicit ethnic gatherings to do this business.

On the mental level, sexual maltreatment is a horrendous mishap: disarray, loss of direction, sensation of defenselessness, passionate stun or mayhem, wave of intense pressure, emergency of importance.

Like any injury, sexual maltreatment can bring about an ongoing condition of post-awful pressure issue.

We should recognize two sorts of mental harm:

The assault of assent, the grown-up forcing on the youngster a conduct to which the last doesn't loan itself; the sensation of blame of the kid, which can be intensified by the directive of the forced mystery.

For the French Federation of Psychiatry, we discuss maltreatment to assign "sexual exercises that he can't comprehend, which are unseemly for his age and his psycho-sexual turn of events". Sexual maltreatment of grown-ups without their assent ought to likewise be accounted for. In the field of neurobiology, the investigation of the outcomes of sexual maltreatment in youth started during the 2000s, and the ends meet towards the exhibit of the obtaining of a complete physiological weakness.

Beginning during the 2000s, a few separate investigations reasoned that youth misuse, especially sexual maltreatment, had authoritative results by actuating a procured weakness that is found in the pressure reaction. The first proof in quite a while dates from 2000, it was proceeded in 2003, and different examinations uncover the dangers of reliance, specifically to liquor, or the dangers of significant burdensome issues (MDD) in 2009.

Turning out to be kid misuse, various examinations authenticate the track of a lower level of pressure chemical (cortisol) on account of maltreatment in youth. This low rate outside of times of pressure brings about a more grounded and diverse reaction to stretch. At the point when this obtained weakness prompts misery, whatever the reason, we start to distinguish a type of sorrow not the same as exemplary gloom, with various responses to a particular stimulant.

At the neurobiological level, a posthumous investigation of casualties who endured maltreatment during adolescence showed an epigenetic guideline of glucocorticoid receptors in the hippocampus connected to the danger of self-destruction in adulthood.

Helpless nations have seen a lot more instances of assault. Notwithstanding the bigoted scourge, there are numerous who exploit minor kids, young ladies, ladies, youthful folks, racialized men for a slice of bread. Sadly the populace is reluctant to reprove these evil intentioned people.

Assault, which concerns any entrance of the person in

question (butt-centric, vaginal, oral), can cause genuine actual harm, contingent upon the youngster's age, actual turn of events and the viciousness of the sly demonstration. In situations where other savagery is related with the sexual maltreatment itself, the minor may endure extra wounds of different sorts.

There are a few sorts of sexual victimizers:

Pedophiles who have a sexual inclination for pre-pubescent youngsters, when they move from dream to rehearse, are ordered as pedophiles or sexual victimizers.

At the point when the inclination concerns kids going through adolescence, it's anything but an issue of pedophilia however of hebephilia, and for pubescent kids, of ephebophilia.

Others feel an instinctual fascination for the person in question, now and again promptly at the hour of current realities: this might be the situation during depraved sexual maltreatment and when the assailant has a generally hetero profile, at last still others are pulled in by mastery. that they can apply on others in the sexual connection, in this way communicating a savage or psychotic part.

Among adoration and disdain, two words recognize, went against on the off chance that you don't cherish somebody so it's the inverse, it's contempt.

You shouldn't constrain somebody to accomplish something they would prefer not to do.

Forestalling separation, bigotry and radicalization is a significant part of coordination.

The battle against all types of separation and brutality, specifically those dependent on beginning or strict association, genuine or assumed, is an essential mission of the School, unequivocally reaffirmed in the law of July 8, 2013. regard for the equivalent respect of individuals, for opportunity of inner voice and secularism are at the core of what the School should show understudies all through their tutoring.

Without a third individual, it isn't ensured. We see during the pandemic, the practices of specific instructors in elementary schools who separate offspring of dark skin tone, putting them a good ways off from offspring of white skin tone.

A motion, a conduct that didn't satisfy countless watchers. The recordings were flowing all over the place and everybody could see it obviously that this is a demonstration of prejudice.

Some posed the inquiry is this a method to secure against one another and if so why, they isolated the kids as a result of their shading.

A Muslim lady, who was denied admittance to the metropolitan pool in a burquini (full bathing suit), looked for guidance from the CFR. To be sure, the guidelines of this public pool disallow the wearing of the burquini.

The CFR audited the content being referred to and discovered the contention for the boycott deficient. It determines that admittance to the pool walled in area was illegal to individuals whose garments denoted a social or strict distinction. In any case, this defense doesn't appear to be clear; it should even be inferred that dress that strays from the typical appearance of the larger part gathering of people is viewed as bothersome. This lady had meanwhile tended to herself straightforwardly to the cooperative; the CFR encouraged him to proceed with this useful exchange.

A Swiss proselyte to Islam moved toward the CFR with respect to the accompanying circumstance: on the event of the progress to auxiliary school, the administration of her little girl's new school coordinated a data meeting for the understudies. Her little girl, who is Muslim and wears the headscarf, joined in. Immediately, the mother got a letter advising her, in addition to other things, that school rules don't permit understudies to have their heads covered during exercises. The young lady actually went to class with her mom, however was not allowed in view of her headscarf. The mother at that point got an admonition that her little girl needed to go to classes without a headscarf and if not, she would need to pay a fine.

The CFR encouraged the mother to keep going with her little girl to class. She had a phone meet with the leader of the educational committee, who was firm and antagonistic to Muslims. Therefore, the CFR encouraged the mother to request a composed choice from the school and afterward challenge the school through an attorney. Upon re-reaching this individual later, the CFR tracked down that the allure against the choice had sadly not prompted the ideal outcome.

The general public of yesterday, today and tomorrow cautions residents to continue in the strides of the experts in power.

On the off chance that you live in a far-off country you ought to be bowing to government orders which appear to be crazy to those concerned.

Each race has their own set, culture and so forth particularly a general public the specialists request to regard the way of life of this region and regularly there is bigotry with respect to unfamiliar societies.

Hatred and Radicalization

Hostile to bigotry and disdain discourse laws will be laws that preclude and forbid separation and disdain discourse, going from terrorizing and denigration to brutality against an individual, a specific classification of the populace or their families. products.

Prompting to racial scorn alludes to calls (composed or oral) of malignant follows up on the alleged or real racial trademark, and disdain discourse alludes to approaches different attributes: religion, age, sex or sexual direction, and so forth .

The expressed point of these laws is to secure against an assault on the qualities on which majority rules system is based, yet additionally to forestall brutality.

We have tracked down that awfully a significant number of our countrymen grumble about the measure of derisive, disparaging, bigot or excusing wrongdoings against humankind without having the option to act successfully against this marvel.

For sure, the control frameworks set up by certain authorities are again and again fragmented and careless. Also, it is the obligation of the specialists to furnish residents with the instruments important for compelling treatment.

Without rebuffing the individuals who have the right to be rebuffed without qualification, if the specialists acknowledged this matter the world has since been in an environment of harmony, love and absolute concordance. Bigots keep on tracking down that most of bigoted demonstrations have not been rebuffed.

A settler survivor of a bigoted demonstration and has nobody to shield him can get mean, radicalist by trying to guard himself.

The battle has scarcely begun we cannot think that this fight is over since the bigots think it is only a game, truth be told imagine an exhibit to dazzle the world.

It's an ideal opportunity to diminish prejudice to tidy!

"That being dark isn't a wrongdoing" and "stopping prejudice" another "pandemic". "Individuals of dark tone are deserted by the individuals who oversee."

The entire world is raising its voice to end prejudice.

Everywhere on the world, exhibitions have occurred all throughout the planet reproving racial segregation. A worldwide development that is joined on the resentment that has set the United States on fire after the demise of George Floyd, a dark American, choked by a white police officer.

From London to Sydney, a great many individuals have overcame the pandemic to end bigotry and police ruthlessness, a remarkable worldwide shock started to request equity for the last mentioned.

In London, overlooking authority removing directions to counter the spread of the new COVID, their countenances covered with a defensive veil for about, many demonstrators accumulated before Parliament, waving signs with the motto "People of color Matter" (Black lives matter). They all yell together in the group.

"The United Kingdom isn't honest", censured the demonstrators in London, drumming drums. As in the British capital, they were various in Manchester (north-west) additionally to march to remind that blacks are people like any person. The demonstrators failed to acknowledge the public authority's various calls to shun partaking due to the wellbeing emergency. They deliberately ignored for a noble motivation.

Australia was quick to commence worldwide shock. A huge number of individuals fought the nation over, waving "I can't inhale" pennants.

For Australian coordinators, in no way, shape or form cooled by the public authority's call to remain at home as a result of the wellbeing emergency, this undertaking discovers many echoes in their country.

In addition, they exploited this stroll to make themselves clear, the awful encounters they had around there.

In Tunis, in excess of 100 individuals requested "equity" and to have the option to "inhale" even with bigotry, which "chokes". "This scourge additionally exists in Tunisia", they are casualties of verbal and actual assaults.

In Liège, in eastern Belgium, 700 individuals resisted the boycott and partook in a walk against bigotry.

In Germany, enemies of bigots have likewise shown their fortitude.

In France as well, the subject of repeating contention as of late, allegations of police brutality combined with those of prejudice have bounced back in the wake of the worldwide shock over the demise of George Floyd. Get-togethers were held to enhance the worldwide development of fortitude against exemption for law requirement.

Notwithstanding, is the scourge no more or is the circumstance today? Recently, today tomorrow, they were the casualty of bigotry, they will in any case be casualties as much as those concerned won't assume their liability by rebuffing the individuals who have the right to be rebuffed.

We are in 2020 and we should stop bigotry. verbal and actual bigotry should be criticized. Eventually, aggregate shock should be utilized to push us ahead as a dark society.

By far most of cops are right, however police bigotry exists, the proof is just excessively. It has happened too often. It is getting ordinary.

Irate African Americans who say that's the last straw. An excess of is excessively, they have manhandled a lot of our shortcomings, our insights, our kindnesses.

For quite a long time, colonialists, soldiers of fortune have abused blacks as though it is their own proprietor, they have obtained with power. It resembles they won the blood, the collection of individuals of color on the front line.

They don't need and don't wish to repudiate the indecencies and customs of the past. Bigots don't care for individuals of color however they like the product of their nursery, their boldness, their solidarity and so on.

In public action, racism is thus assimilated in priority to ideas, prejudices, ideologies, speeches or even hostile attitudes and acts of violence that must be combated through education or penalization.

The assimilation of racism to the expression of hatred of others and to forms of verbal or physical aggression or violence based on membership (real or imaginary) to a group or a population is shared by racialized social subjects and discriminated against...

The segregative orientation of post-war urban policies is evident in the United States, where the concept of "institutional racism" is adequately applied, understood as the silent permeation into the functioning of institutions of goals and objectives representations that reproduce and exacerbate racial inequalities.

In broad daylight activity, bigotry is in this way acclimatized in need to thoughts, biases, belief systems, talks or even antagonistic mentalities and demonstrations of brutality that should be battled through training or punishment.

The digestion of prejudice to the outflow of contempt of others and to types of verbal or actual animosity or brutality dependent on enrollment (genuine or non-existent) to a gathering or a populace is shared by racialized social subjects and victimized...

The segregative direction of post-war metropolitan strategies is clear in the United States, where the idea of "institutional bigotry" is sufficiently applied, comprehended as the quiet pervasion into the working of establishments of objectives and targets. portrayals that imitate and intensify racial disparities.

To stop the dying, we should initially join together. Without association, we can not the slightest bit add to the difference in this general public and guarantee that everybody has the privilege to make the most of their life in complete opportunity.

However, confronted with the scourge of the bigoted which consistently introduces itself as a test and an inconsistency any individual who regards himself can neither acknowledge nor stroll in this rationale of predominance of both.

Furthermore, to stop this wonder, we have a few choices: Direct a mindfulness crusade, spur individuals to lasting social occasions to demonstrate reality. Sharpen youngsters not to feel embarrassed or dismissed by bigoted society. Put stock in their latent capacity.

Love their skin tone. On the off chance that we just trust that a couple of episodes will act, this commitment truly amounts to nothing. To end bigotry we should utilize every one of the apparatuses that can fill in as a key driver.

To accomplish this we need individuals, donors, warriors willing and resolved to remove this scourge.

Prejudice and bigotry are serious issues in totally debilitated social orders, likewise an abnormality, a test for majority rule government.

We can utilize a wide range of sports to do an enemy of prejudice mindfulness crusade. Television, radio, web-based media spots, banners and so forth.

Everybody can make their own foundation to unite, sharpen, spur youthful and old each one of the individuals who have terrible data about the existence of any person on earth.

Show them that nobody is better than another paying little mind to their political colleague, their fortune, their positions, their identity, their starting point, their race and so on.

Because of the activism of associations, some certain progressions in the battle against prejudice. In any case, there is even more to do.

The discussion and the battle can't end as long as foundational prejudice is as yet present in establishments and racialized casualties are as yet minimized.

You envision that you were in the spot of the people in question, there is no getting away from it: the casualties are for the most part outsiders without assistance.

Do you know why the bigoted scourge is going full speed ahead? Essentially on the grounds that the specialists don't attempt the hoodlums.

Furthermore, also, the absence of inspiration of the dependable staff is expanding step by step for explicit reasons.

A representative of hostile to separation administrations isn't really a non-bigoted individual. Most of cases shut were focused by friendly specialists.

This conduct unmistakably shows that they are against taking care of this issue.

Notwithstanding the endeavors of enemies of bigots to kill this worldwide scourge which is equivalent to COVID-19, the counter changes would prefer not to see a world in harmony without battle, in delight.

Without adjusting things we are totally trapped in a snare of imbalance of people of the world. it is that we are generally people, homos sapiens and that in this manner we are totally established similarly.

However, what makes us all unique is that we don't have similar preferences, similar characters and a similar childhood.

We additionally have an alternate build: some are tall, slender, fat, with blue, green, earthy colored, dark eyes, dark, white skin, and so on.

We dissect our day by day benefit.

We are all the same because we were all born on the same Earth, the same way. We are dust and we will turn dust.

We all have the same way of being born and growing up: from babies to adults.

The difference we do not have the same tastes, the same habits, the same ideas, the same education no matter how similar we each are unique.

The world would be strange if we all looked the same, it would be impossible for everyone to do the same thing without competition.

The entire human body is made up: a body, arms, legs, fingers, a head...

Our characteristic points are different because we do not all react in the same way.

All of us born in a mother's womb, we have been babies, children, adolescents, and adults. We are all indiscriminately human beings.

Even if some have similarities, resemblances, different tastes, different ideas. A world where everyone was the same would be a boring world, unsurprisingly.

The Role of Relevant Agencies

For a long time now, this assistance administration for casualties and outsiders has become a position of reference in issue of outsiders' privileges and legitimate guide against prejudice and segregation: gathering, tuning in, support, exhortation, case building, assuagement, intercession, and at times lawful activity.

Notwithstanding singular help to casualties, it is likewise an issue of educating and sharpening individuals and their company on their privileges, just as on the working of equity, police powers, and so on, in the intend to give the information and perspectives essential for their liberation and the activity of their social rights.

The social and legitimate area often intercedes for the association of working gatherings, assembly or backing for dissident activities, by giving its aptitude (cooperatives of Sans-Papier, activity against shut focuses, and so forth). This area is additionally liable for checking advancements in enemy of segregation and refuge enactment and approaches. For this, he drives the MRAX Legal Commission, comprised of volunteer legal counselors.

According to some people to fight racism, for example in the classroom, there are various ways of making the classroom a place of acceptance and integration between races. Students' reactions depend on cultural factors, such as their level of acceptance of eye contact, their receptiveness to group teaching, or the way they tell a story or act out a scene. If there is a racial conflict in the classroom, it should be approached frankly, without trying to sidestep it.

Teach students to recognize behaviors that can reinforce racism. Study the lives of famous people who fought against discrimination.

Talk about the contribution of men and women around the world to the common fund of knowledge and wisdom of mankind.

Introduce as much human diversity as possible into the curriculum: Ask students' parents and families, or their friends, to help you in this area. Invite people of other races or colors who are actively involved in the life of the community to come and talk about it in class.

Ask students to envision a multiracial society where they will have to live without knowing in advance what color their skin will be.

The notion of "minority group" is often confused with that of "ethnic" group and, often, with that of "race". The term "minority group" is rather vague and is also used to refer to indigenous populations, displaced populations, migrant workers, refugees, and even oppressed majorities. What all these groups have in common is often poverty. A minority group can cease to be one if it becomes powerful enough.

Members of minority groups have individual rights, but they also usually claim certain collective rights as members of the group. Depending on the case, this will be the right to self-determination (cultural and political), the right to land, the right to reparation (in the event of expropriation), the right to inspect natural resources or the right to land access to religious sites.

Identification of certain "minority groups" help students

define what are "minority groups": Is it still a digital minority? How do minorities generally differ from the rest of the population?

Collecting all of the students' suggestions, make a list of contemporary "minority groups", starting with the local community. Do not forget about minorities based on social origin, skills, sexual orientation and other non-racial factors. Do these minorities suffer from discrimination? In what way?

Older pupils could do case studies to determine the importance, area of settlement, history, culture, living conditions and main demands of certain minority groups.

The Role of Anti-discrimination

You need to recognize yourself from a social perspective. We as a whole have a social personality, in spite of the fact that we are not generally mindful of it, since it is a basic piece of us. In any case, in nations with ethnic, strict, etymological or native minorities, the issue of social character regularly emerges regarding regard for common freedoms, particularly when people with great influence guarantee to force their way of life on them. minority gatherings.

The Convention on the Rights of the Child gives specific consideration to one side of the youngster to their social character. Article 29 ensures youngsters training which imparts in them regard for their language and social qualities. Article 30 specifically perceives the privilege of native youngsters, or kids having a place with minority gatherings, to have their own social life and to rehearse their religion or to utilize their own language and article 31 perceives the option to take an interest. completely to social and imaginative life.

The UNESCO Universal Declaration on Cultural Diversity (2 November 2001) underlines, in its first article, the connection among personality and social variety: "Culture takes different structures across existence. This variety is exemplified in the inventiveness and majority of personalities that describe the gatherings and social orders that make up humankind. A wellspring of trade, advancement and inventiveness, social variety is, for humanity, as fundamental as biodiversity in the request for living things."

Study your own local area: Are there social minorities? Is their way of life regarded? Do their individuals take an interest openly and out in the open in the social exercises of their local area, or is it felt that they ought to do as such in private or not in the slightest degree? There are some schools support regard for the way of life of minorities?

After a long time after week individuals are embarrassed, offended and beaten due to bigotry in the Brandenburg area. This viciousness influences certain gatherings of individuals specifically: for instance, the individuals who come from a country other than Germany, yet in addition vagrants, individuals of color, Jews, gay people, transsexual individuals, activists of left, individuals with inabilities or elective teenagers from equal societies. The message behind this viciousness is clear: You are not wanted here, you don't have anything to do here!

Those influenced are normally individuals from minority bunches who as such regularly endure segregation consistently. This segregation comes from the actual heart of society. It meddles in the most ordinary irreverence and debasing looks, yet in addition in prohibitive changes of the privilege to haven, for example, being put in a convenience place, the preclusion to work or the reality of not approaching all friendly advantages as an evacuee.

On the off chance that we banter in the papers or in nearby bistros about the alleged "danger" that movement addresses from one viewpoint for the inward security of the host nations and then again the presence of vagrants and troublemakers and their hurtful results on the travel industry and the economy, the limit traditional gatherings consider until the present time that they are just doing what individuals truly need.

The demonstration of brutality is frequently capable quickly by casualties as an embarrassing encounter. Bigoted viciousness is typically not aimed at the casualty's individual specifically. In this way, casualties are not assaulted due to their conduct, but since they will be doled out to a specific class of individuals. Individuals around them likewise feel focused by this brutality. They realize this is for them as well. This along these lines produces a ton of dread among family members. In the most pessimistic scenario, the people in question, similar to the expected survivors of their escort, pull out from social and public life and surprisingly come to keep away from certain public places, for example, stops or train stations.

Regardless, the casualties by and large and time and again stay all alone. They frequently experience when they tell current realities and rather than the normal help, suspicious looks if not the pretty much direct allegation of having caused the actual episode. Now and again they will be alluded to as the actual attacker. Really dear companions and family members will in general make light of current realities: "It wasn't so terrible!"

Individuals concerned, not inclination viewed appropriately, for this situation experience a subsequent physical issue. What suits the aggressors. Undoubtedly, when residents, social specialists, guardians, passers-by stay uninvolved, turn away from the scene and leave the person in question(s) alone, the bigoted aggressors acquire in power. Allow us to remain rather unmistakably and transparently for the people in question and next to them to show our fortitude and backing them notwithstanding viciousness!

Anti-racism Propaganda

I demand the earnestness to go about as fast as could really be expected, the specialists, associations and affiliations should do everything possible, utilize all way to stop this scourge which slaughters individuals quietly and subtly. Also, to recognize what should be done to assemble the most ideal future.

The European Union is involved with the United Nations Convention on the Rights of Persons with Disabilities and the European Parliament assumes a significant part in advancing, defending and observing the use of the show by the Union. Battle against prejudice and xenophobia. The European Parliament is preparing to battle bigotry and xenophobia. In any case, for what reason is the quantity of cases not diminishing however expanding? Who is accountable for this significant subject? It persistently approaches the Union and its Member States to take measures to forestall bigotry and xenophobia and to battle these scourges through training, by advancing a culture of regard and resilience.

To stop the dying, we should initially join together. Without association, we can not the slightest bit add to the difference in this general public and guarantee that everybody has the privilege to make the most of their life in complete opportunity.

In any case, confronted with the scourge of bigotry which consistently introduces itself as a test and an inconsistency, any individual who regards himself can neither acknowledge nor stroll in this rationale of prevalence over each other.

Also, to stop this wonder, we have a few alternatives, to do a mindfulness crusade, to inspire individuals to a lasting get-together to demonstrate the truth.

In the event that we just trust that a couple of episodes will deny the plague, the work will not be done nor finished. We should discuss it and yell uproariously until the last arrangements.

Through the discourses of certain authorities, they affirm their good faith and the significance of gaining from recorded shameful acts to pursue fabricating an enduring harmony.

It is essential to comprehend the elements of rejection and misuse in our social orders, without the solidarity of the current battle against separation all throughout the planet, by underscoring activities like the International Coalition of Cities Against Racism, which advances participation and joint effort in the battle against segregation broadly and universally.

"Basic freedoms reach out to everybody, and we should continually work with the goal that everybody realizes their commitment to work for the end of prejudice." According to a Canadian city center position.

I comprehend the readiness of the propelled specialists keen on tackling the issue of prejudice, which is a scourge, however the actions taken as I would see it are not very compelling.

Yet, I promise you, the day they choose to stop the expression "bigotry" it will be managed with no vagueness.

They have all the essential gear, gadgets helpful to reestablish harmony, love, the great climate to ensure the admiration of each person.

To guarantee that everybody's privileges and opportunities are regarded, the Defender of Rights has two methods for activity: from one perspective, he manages the individual solicitations he gets in law and on the other, he completes special activities. correspondence.

The Defender of Rights is an establishment free of the State. Made in 2011 and cherished in the Constitution, it has been endowed with two missions: to protect individuals whose rights are not regarded; permit everybody to have equivalent admittance to rights.

The Defender of Rights expects to battle prejudice. It's an obvious fact that the quantity of public authorities accepting that they have been survivors of in any event one separation or good provocation dependent on an oppressive ground with regards to their expert movement, following consistent increment since the demise of George Floyd in May 2020, presently arrives at a level!

Practices, obviously unbiased, producing segregation. Different benefits would likewise be normal from the presentation of such a cure: an individual way to deal with restitution to assist a solitary casualty due with the impact restricted to the gatherings to a preliminary of res judicata. we would move to an aggregate way to deal with prosecution for all casualties in a comparable circumstance, any individual whose circumstance meets the models set out to characterize the referent gathering who can join the activity; in light of a legitimate concern for the great organization of equity, such a class activity would make it conceivable to restrict the quantity of activities by consolidating them; most importantly, the mass impact would make this sort of activity more dissuasive on the grounds that the sums included would be more prominent than the punishments accommodated by the correctional code (see above) and then those at present dispensed by the adjudicators for harms; such cures would hence have preventive just as severe and compensatory temperance.

To battle against immediate or aberrant separation, of which public authorities are regularly focused on, the protectors of the free established specialists organized by natural law n ° 2011-333 of March 29, 2011 have assembled huge insightful forces. It is endowed to gather the data important for the achievement of its assignments from the respondents. Today, in 2020, and in spite of every one of its vows to safeguards, the issue isn't yet settled. It happens that a large portion of those accountable for tending to or taking care of this issue are against this significant change. Pietism should have its place in a climate loaded proudly and unending bedlam. Equity is indivisible from a special case and a subject of concern. Confronted with separation or gathering, casualties have total opportunity to document an objection.

The common freedoms safeguard additionally utilizes every one of his forces of intercession: toward the finish of the examination of the objection and when the separation is set up, he utilizes the most fitting arrangement, regardless of whether it is to determine the grumbling. Genially the debate, to intervene, to define a proposition for an answer, or to introduce an assessment to the managerial court. The arrangement picked relies upon the desire of the candidate, the presence of a legitimate cure, the circumstance to be confronted (assurance of the delegate actually existing, move, and so on) and as far as possible. While safeguards have made a move, they likewise depend intensely on advancing correspondence. We are a long way from the real world and the issue exists.

The mission depended by article 34 of the previously

mentioned natural law has assumed a fundamental part in the anticipation of segregation, specifically by assisting public businesses with carrying out dynamic strategies positive for correspondence. Be that as it may, in 2020 we are seeing the ascent of prejudice. The public area of ethnic minorities is a long way from invulnerable to plummet based separation. These can intercede during enrollment and bigotry is ubiquitous out in the open and private associations.

Mission Action by Safeguards

Pursuant to Organic Law No. 2011-333 of 29 March 2011 on basic liberties safeguards, basic freedoms protectors have a wide scope of insightful forces, the extent of which incorporates the option to demand a clarification, which can be settled by hearing the respondent if vital. With the help of a legal counselor (Article 18), and if vital, complete ban on location assessment under the management of an adjudicator (Article 22). however, the privacy of the examination isn't kept secret, or classification can't be summoned (Article 20). On the off chance that he doesn't wish to do as such, the safeguard can give a conventional notification or allude the case to a synopsis judge (article 21). To determine questions, common freedoms protectors have different apparatuses. He would, thus, be able to intercede upstream, to forestall a question, regardless of whether via proposals, specifically of impartial settlement (article 25), intercession with a view to the friendly goal of debates (article 26) or settlement (article 28). Reference to the Defender of Rights doesn't, in any case, suspend the limit time frames (article 6).

With regards to a debate, the Defender of Rights may intercede before common, authoritative or criminal courts, either in line with the court or of a gathering, or on his own drive, which addresses a striking explicitness (article 33).

Notwithstanding his typical forces of examination and debate settlement, the Defender of Rights has explicit privileges in the battle against separation.

In any case, it very well may be seized by reason of this ability not just by any individual who sees himself as the casualty of segregation, immediate or roundabout, or by his recipients, yet in addition, "By any affiliation consistently announced for at any rate five years. a long time on the date of the realities proposing by its rules to battle separation or to help survivors of segregation, mutually with the individual believing himself to be the casualty of separation or with his understanding."

Besides, the Defender of Rights acquired from the Halde his central goal of helping an individual who views himself as a casualty of separation in the constitution of his case and in the selection of methodology adjusted to his case, in the event that he thinks about that the grumbling requires a mediation on his part, as per article 27 of natural law n ° 2011-333 of March 29, 2011 referenced previously. Article 37 of a similar natural law likewise engages the specialists of the Defender of Rights to do tests (cf. Supra).

Thirdly, the Defender of Rights can suggest that a public position utilize its forces of suspension or assent against a characteristic or lawful individual subject to its endorsement or approval in case of a finding of segregation, in use of article 30 of this equivalent natural law.

Finally, article 28 of this equivalent natural law accommodates a unique method of debate settlement: the exchange in criminal issue.

Like the Halde before him, the Defender of Rights was enabled to propose to the creator of acts establishing segregation inside the significance of the reformatory code an exchange comprising in the installment of a fine of a sum not which may surpass 3,000 euros for a characteristic individual and 15,000 euros for a legitimate individual, joined where proper by a promoting measure. If there should arise an occurrence of acknowledgment by the creator of current realities and, if essential, by the person in question, the exchange should be affirmed by the public investigator. Accordingly, the execution of the exchange interferes with the restriction time frame and its execution quenches the public activity; notwithstanding, it doesn't subvert the casualty's entitlement to acquire common pay under the steady gaze of the criminal court.

In case of refusal of the exchange or non-execution of an acknowledged and affirmed exchange, then again, the Defender of Rights can start public activity by direct summons. At the point when current realities before the Defender of Rights lead to a primer or blatant examination, the assent of the public investigator should be gotten preceding any exchange by excellence of article 23 of the natural law.

Nonetheless, in spite of the resumption by the Defender of Rights of the multitude of missions and privileges of the Halde, the rapporteurs could just note the expansive agreement of individuals heard during the consultation lamenting the shift to the foundation of the battle against separation.

On the side of this affirmation is regularly advanced the drop in the quantity of references to the Defender of Rights for the battle against segregation contrasted with references to the Halde, in spite of what has been noticed for the protection of youngsters or the morals of safety, recommending a lot sifting of solicitations.

The primary driver would be a deficiency of perceivability of the Defender of Rights according to the Halde because of an absence of correspondence during the consolidation of the specialists. The Defender of Rights would in this way be seen more as a super-Mediator instead of as additionally the replacement of the Halde, so the scene of authoritative specialists would hereafter do not have a body equipped for managing the issue of separation.

Nonetheless, Mr. Richard Senghor likewise focused on that there was, in total terms, a low number of references for separation, specifically on grounds of cause, identity, race or religion, regardless of whether it is the Defender of Rights or the courts. He added that this low rate didn't mirror the truth of segregation in France.

The mission of elevating uniformity depended to the Defender of Rights by Article 34 of the Organic Law of March 29, 2011 is indivisible from his central goal of securing casualties of separation.

Shockingly, the mission depended to the Defenders of Rights appears to be an unthinkable or bombed mission or troublesome because of the way that the level of individuals concerned are blood bigots.

To get a new line of work, most of cases depend on her skin tone, her race and regularly a white candidate is bound to get a new line of work quicker than a dark one.

At the assistance of the public authority, it plans to decipher the officially declared uniformity into training, by forestalling separation and by supporting the execution by open managers of dynamic approaches for correspondence.

In contrast to the treatment of individual protests, the advancement of fairness depends primarily on an investigation of practices to set up fundamental activities over the long haul, prone to make them advance.

The European Parliament has passed laws to disallow a wide range of segregation, anyway the scourge is surely present wherever on the planet and in all individuals are equivalent under the steady gaze of the law, denies any separation, situated specifically on sex, race, shading, ethnic or social causes, hereditary attributes, language, religion or convictions, political assessments or some other assessment, participation of a public minority , birth, incapacity, age or sexual direction.

Denying all separation and defending basic rights are two of the mainstays of the Union's lawful request. Regardless of this, specific gatherings keep on confronting segregation in the Union.

The European Parliament is activating to determine this issue and advance correspondence in EU law and arrangements.

Uniformity among ladies and men is a key estimation of the European Union.

The European Parliament assumes a vital part in supporting the arrangement of sex equity and equivalent freedoms, especially through its Committee on Women's Rights and Gender Equality and by advancing the coordination of sex fairness issues in crafted by its councils and assignments.

Privileges of people with inabilities:

The Union perceives and regards the privilege of people with inabilities to profit by measures intended to guarantee their freedom, social and word related combination and interest in the existence of the local area.

1. Equality: it implies giving exactly the same thing to everybody.

2. Fairness: being reasonable in each activity.

Bad form, any place it happens, is a danger to equity wherever else, for we are completely up to speed in a snare of shared relations. – Martin Luther King Jr.

Regardless of the endeavors of certain associations to battle bigotry all over the place, yet this doesn't forestall the expansion in instances of casualties of prejudice.

Consistently we praise the International Day for the Elimination of Racial Discrimination, in Alabama (United States of America), perhaps the most significant urban areas on the planet in the battle against bigotry yet doesn't forestall the rate high prejudice.

A youthful Swiss of shading is doing a one-week temporary job, as a component of the expert joining program, as a server in a café. Toward the finish of the entry level position, he doesn't get the apprenticeship place. The temporary position report applauds the nature of his work, and yet the business says he likes to employ a "Heidi".

He says, "Clients can't be approached to acknowledge his appearance." The schoolmaster went to the CFR. The adolescent likewise looked for exchange with the business, with the help of his instructor. After the main explanations got by the CFR and a first lawful assessment, the CFR lost contact. The young person would not like to keep battling in view of the racial segregation he had encountered.

A hued man goes to a club on a Saturday night. At the passage, the custodian checks his reports and afterward denies him access. A similar situation just unfurled with another shaded man.

A colleague of the casualty impugned the case to the CFR, determining that the last had effectively had a similar encounter a few times. Disavowal of access regularly can't be demonstrated. This is the reason it is critical to discover observers who noticed the scene. The CFR encouraged the casualty to record an objection.

Conclusion

On the planet there is just one race: "it is mankind". We don't reserve the privilege to be founded on actual contrasts, identity, starting point, nationality, skin tone, facial highlights, stature and so on.

We can not be the slightest bit envision, imagine that some are better than others until isolating mankind in a various leveled way, in other words by thinking about that there are better men analyzed than different men than we would place in a lower class.

All in all, we reserve no option to accept, and particularly to pretend, that since we are white skin that we have extra characteristics contrasted with an individual of the shade of dark.

We are largely equivalent, we as a whole have blood a similar tone as we have pink, white, dark earthy colored or even yellow skin. Nobody can embarrass someone else on the affection of significance and predominance. everybody has the privilege to a glad existence with pride.

Every one of the individuals who try to legitimize bigotry on the social side are committing a genuine error. I notice that on schedule and in measures, the combinations of blood progress quickly.

Numerous outsiders share their life intently or remotely starting with one soil then onto the next, they are joined together and resolved to live respectively always regardless of the law of the two nations put an obstruction in their middle.

In doing as such, it is even more stressing for what it's worth at the core of significant patterns, which are those of the social and social fracture of our social orders.

The more specific social characters create, ethnic, strict, "sex", and so forth, the more the possibility of nation withdraws to partake in a responsive populism or be decreased to a patriotism which the limit conservatives feed on, and the more the space of prejudice is reestablished and reached out, for its dominatingly differentialist variants. We should know that whatever advancements may occur, almost certainly, our social orders will be progressively enticed by bigotry.

This will establish to an ever increasing extent if not a discernible reality, in any event a test, a danger in every case prone to emerge and spread: in the conflict of characters, and their unending cycles of disintegration and recomposition; in the powerlessness of our social entertainers to remake clashes and hence friendly relations as organizing as those which went against the laborers' development to the experts of work in the prime of industry; in the weaknesses, disappointments and emergency of our foundations, states and political frameworks.

Yet, these stressing possibilities additionally have their positive side, in light of the fact that similar elements, which work toward developing bigotry, go in that of a fortifying of undermined or focused on gatherings...

What I don't understand is that all the international black celebrities don't take this issue very seriously, they are always waiting to complain, if they are a victim or an international issue like the George Floyd case, you can see their frustration. But why have they never taken this issue to heart to find a solution to end racism permanently? (changes made)

I said indeed, and I immovably trust in it together we can dispense with this scourge, the arrangement is around the colonizers, since the thought of race has its source in subjection and imperialism. They are the ones who are established in the idea of race in bondage and imperialism. They are the ones who hold the way in to the entryway open to all by learning and tolerating to live respectively. Also, it will be programmed, we will have a world without war and scorn, however, encompassed by harmony and love. Allow us to save humankind, let us together take out the scourge of bigotry.